True Worship

True Worship

JUSTIN MILLER

WIPF & STOCK · Eugene, Oregon

TRUE WORSHIP

Copyright © 2020 Justin Miller. All rights reserved. Except for brief quotations in critical publications or reviews, no part of this book may be reproduced in any manner without prior written permission from the publisher. Write: Permissions, Wipf and Stock Publishers, 199 W. 8th Ave., Suite 3, Eugene, OR 97401.

Wipf & Stock
An Imprint of Wipf and Stock Publishers
199 W. 8th Ave., Suite 3
Eugene, OR 97401

www.wipfandstock.com

PAPERBACK ISBN: 978-1-5326-8730-3
HARDCOVER ISBN: 978-1-5326-8731-0
EBOOK ISBN: 978-1-5326-8732-7

Manufactured in the U.S.A.   April 22, 2020

To my God. Your covenantal love is better than life and your majesty seen clearly in Holy Scripture is my heart's desire all because of your kind sovereign grace to this unworthy wretch.

Table of Contents

Acknowledgments ix

1 Regulative Worship—God is the Object and Consumer of Worship 1

2 Two Testaments, Same Message—Old 21

3 Two Testaments, Same Message—New 33

4 True Worship of God in Spirit and Truth 47

APPENDIX 1: Service Orders of Regulative Worship Churches 73

APPENDIX 2: Recommended Resources for Further Study 77

Bibliography 79

Acknowledgement

JoDawn, thank you for all you do for our family. Your loving sacrifice makes ministry possible and you share in all that God is doing in that work. Kaleb, Ella, Isaac, and Eden, I pray that you live out your created purpose to glorify God and enjoy him forever. He alone is all satisfying. He alone is worthy of all your worship.

I

Regulative Worship—God Is the Object and Consumer of Worship

DEUT 12:32

32 *Whatever I command you, you shall be careful to do; you shall not add to nor take away from it.*[1]

MATT 28:16-20

16 But the eleven disciples proceeded to Galilee, to the mountain which Jesus had designated. **17** When they saw Him, they worshiped Him; but some were doubtful. **18** And Jesus came up and spoke to them, saying, "All authority has been given to Me in heaven and on earth. **19** Go therefore and make disciples of all the nations, baptizing them in the name of the Father and the Son and the Holy Spirit, **20** *teaching them to observe all that I commanded you*; and lo, I am with you always, even to the end of the age."[2]

MAKE SURE EVERYTHING IS done per the rules. That philosophy was the essence of my first job out of graduate school. My job was an auditor and my job description revolved around auditing the financial statements, business processes, and controls of the business units of the company I worked for. An auditor at a very basic level is making sure the company is operating per its own set principles as well as the governmental rules. As a young professional I observed the reality of the business world I had come into as an auditor, that the company is ultimately ruled by its shareholders as the "owners" of the company and they dictate the end for which the company exists. Not only did the shareholders dictate the mission of the company but the exact means for its operation to that end. They dictated the mission and the methodology of the company. When the methodology was not kept, people were reprimanded and some lost their jobs. The company was to run in the exact manner as the shareholders had organized. The whole thesis of this book revolves around the reality that the triune God is the sole shareholder of his creation and his redeemed people. Therefore, he dictates the end to which they exist (his glory) and the means by which they are to live unto him (worship him per his word).

Mankind, God's chief creation, made in God's image, is commanded to worship God per his methodology to the end that we reflect back to him his glory. We were created to worship God and enjoy him forever. We, all from Adam per Rom 5:12, failed in the garden of Eden when Adam ate from the forbidden tree. We all as human beings have failed ever since (Rom 3:23) and even willfully trade the worship of the Creator for the creation (Rom 1:22–25). God decreed to allow the fall to ultimately display the fullness of his attributes in a fallen world which finds its climax in the redemptive work of the Lord Jesus on the cross. The cross of the Lord Jesus is the means whereby God purchased a people for himself, a people forgiven of all our failure, to worship him and honor him. The redeemed of God are the forgiven of God by the Lord Jesus being the perfect sinless sacrifice in our place whereby the Lord Jesus (who is truly God and man per John 1:1, 14) took our punishment so that we may have his perfect track record before God (2 Cor 5:21). In Christ all those God set his eternal will on have the penalty for their sin paid by the perfect life of Jesus culminating in his death in their place on a rugged tree. The Lord Jesus Christ rising from the dead validated his person and work. His ascension forty days afterward returned him to the glory he shared with the Father before his incarnation. Fallen man cannot properly worship God until God himself brings them back into fellowship with himself. The Lord Jesus accomplished that end for God's beloved people, those who turn from sin and trust in the Lord Jesus alone for salvation. The redeemed of God are those ultimately saved by God the Father through the work of the Son of God on the cross, applied by the Spirit of God who indwells God's people producing in them repentance and faith, all to the end that they are worshippers of God forever.

The primary function of the Christian who has been born of the Holy Spirit is to be a worshipper of God in spirit and truth (John 4:24). The Christian is called as a redeemed person to personally and as part of a local church ascribe to God honor, praise, and glory due to his name (1 Cor 10:31, Heb 10:23–25). What does that look like? What exactly is worship? How is God to be worshipped by his people? In the coming pages we explore those questions in order to see what the *true worship* of God is.

God is the Consumer and Object of Worship

God is the consumer of worship. God is the object of genuine and authentic worship. These two truths lead us inevitably to the conclusion that since God is the consumer and object of worship then he alone defines what worship is and governs how it is to be done. Psalm 95:6 states, "Come, let us worship and bow down, Let us kneel before the LORD our Maker." The phrase "let us worship" is the translation of the Hebrew word "hwh," which means, "bow down, prostrate oneself, bowing lowing in act of honor and reverence."[3] Worship is responding with reverential awe and joyful submission to all that God is as seen in all that God has said (his word) and done (his works). Another way of defining worship

---

3. Swanson, *Dictionary of Biblical Languages*.

biblically is that worship is "the praise, adoration and reverence of God, both in public and private. It is a celebration of the worthiness of God, by which honour is given to his name."[4] Worship is the celebration of God's attributes and glory. It is the adoration of a life enamored with God's majestic glory. God is the consumer/object of worship and he defines worship and sets the terms for how he is to be approached in adoration and praise. He sets the terms and gives the instructions concerning how to honor him. How to celebrate and attribute to him glory. *True worship* is a response to the Word and works of God whereby we adore him with all our affections and ascribe to him honor and praise with our minds and wills. The psalmist in Ps 150 shows the essence of worship by penning the following:

> Praise the LORD!
> Praise God in His sanctuary;
> Praise Him in His mighty expanse.
> Praise Him for His mighty deeds;
> Praise Him according to His excellent greatness.
>
> Praise Him with trumpet sound;
> Praise Him with harp and lyre.
> Praise Him with timbrel and dancing;
> Praise Him with stringed instruments and pipe.
> Praise Him with loud cymbals;
> Praise Him with resounding cymbals.
> Let everything that has breath praise the LORD.
> Praise the LORD!

Worship is our response to God's glory as God's redeemed whereby we praise and adore him! In order to do that rightly we must understand that the same Scripture that tells us about the God to adore tells all of us how to adore him.

---

4. Manser, *Zondervan Dictionary of Bible Themes*.

The Worship of God is Regulated by God's Word

Moses in his instructions to the people of Israel stated in Deut 12:32, "Whatever I command you, you shall be careful to do; you shall not add to nor take away from it." He reminds them that his commands are to govern how they live and worship him both individually and corporately as his people. God had redeemed them from bondage in Egypt. They were to be careful to do all that God had said and not add to or take away from it. Moses is saying to them worship God per his instructions in the Word and do not veer away from the Word of God to the slightest. To not veer away from the Word is something Moses understood well in his interaction with God on Mt. Sinai. God told Moses in Exod 25:9, "According to all that I am going to show you, *as* the pattern of the tabernacle and the pattern of all its furniture, just so you shall construct *it*." Moses was told by God to build the tabernacle exactly as God had shown him. If God cared that much about how cloth was to be arranged in symbolic representation of his throne room how can we ever think that God would not care concerning how we worship him each day or as we gather together as his people? He told Moses to make the tabernacle exactly as he has shown him. He conveys to us that we are to worship him exactly as he has commanded us. Worship that does not conform to his commands is not *true worship*.

In the bringing forth of the new covenant our Lord Jesus upheld the importance of following/worshipping him per his commands. In the Great Commission Jesus instructs his apostles to teach those who follow Jesus as disciples to observe (observing meaning to obey) his (Christ's) commands (Matt 28:19-20). Jesus redeemed his people from their slavery to sin and the penalty of sin unto the end that they would learn his commands and heed them as worshippers of the One True God in Spirit (being born again) and in Truth (knowing Jesus who is epitome of God's revelation to man). The church/elect of God are redeemed to worship God through Jesus by the power the Holy Spirit supplies per the commands of God. God regulates his worship. He dictates to us how we are to live, what we are to do, and how we are to assemble as his people all to the end of ascribing honor to his name and celebrating his infinite worth. *God's commands simultaneously are also for our greatest good* per Moses to the people in Deut 10:12–13 and Jesus in Matt 11:28–30. God's commands are not for our harm but for our good as we fulfill our created purpose to worship God and enjoy him forever. One of the greatest threats to the modern church and professing Christians is how we approach God in worship. There are two overarching principles that churches and people follow in our time whether they realize it or not. The first principle that most today follow is the normative principle. The other principle is called the regulative principle.

Normative Principle

The normative principle states that if something is not forbidden by the Word of God it is okay to do in the worship of God, particularly in the local church gathering. The normative principle views the law of God as a line in the sand, which we can tip toe close to but should never cross. This principle views the Word of God's commands as a fence that must be stayed within. The Word of God is a guide for the Christian in the worship of God.

Regulative Principle

The regulative principle states that we only do what the Word of God explicitly commands or provides an example of with regards to the worship of God, particularly in the local church gathering. The regulative principle sees the Word of God as what governs every aspect of our lives. Just as the government oversees the lives of the citizens under its authority so the regulative principle sees the Word of God as the government of the lives of Christians which are to be lived entirely unto the worship of the triune God. The regulative principle is rooted in the reality of the sufficiency of

Scripture. The Word of God governs the Christian in the worship of God.

To understand the importance of this in light of the all-seeing gaze of the Lord Jesus permit me tell you the story of two churches (fictional churches gathered from examples of many churches I know), both that make the claim that they each Sunday come together to worship God. Let us take a moment and look at these two churches from the perspective of you attending these churches and let us also, whether true or not, imagine that you have a limited background with Christianity. You decide to attend the two following fictional churches on consecutive Sundays. The first church is Relevant Church and the second Sunday you visit Spirit and Truth Church.

The Normative Church (Relevant Church)

Relevant Church is the buzz of the region. Their seats are filled each and every Sunday. They have many services and even several campuses where they broadcast their charismatic and well-known preacher via a large screen in the sanctuary. They have the best kids program available and nursery with state-of-the-art sign-in technology as well as professional staff to ensure your kids are taken to the right place and class. They market the theme that they are a church for everyone. They have a Starbucks coffee bar, a café, couple of shops at the main campus, and really nice non-churchy looking buildings for their main as well as other campuses. When you come into one of the worship services, one of many in various locations, one of their pastors greets all from the stage with, "How are you feeling today?" They make some announcements and tell you about all the neat things coming up that week. That Sunday they have several baptisms. They bring them in the baptistry and ask them if they have received Jesus. They communicate that anyone can get baptized but they have to arrive before service and turn in a card. After the baptisms are done then all of a sudden the lights go out. The stage, which is very modernly decorated, lights up, and smoke arises at the end of the stage. The atmosphere is electric and the praise band much like a rock band comes on the stage and begins to sing. People's hands are up as they sing about how they will follow God and how he will bless them. The music quality is professionally astute. They use even secular songs they have "redeemed" that can be, from the right perspective, about God. Songs with moving melodies and engaging humanistic lyrics. All you can hear is the band playing and the singer singing. The lyrics are emotionally charging. The lyrics are repetitive combined with a growing tempo that heightens your emotional experience. At the end of the performance the singers come down as a video is shown on the screen conveying the overarching message of the sermon series the preaching pastor is in that week. The lights brighten a tad bit but overall it is still dark in the sanctuary with just the stage lit up. The preaching pastor gets up, tells a joke or two, and then moves onto officially open his messaging by telling a great story with a motivational theme. He then reads a couple of Scriptures and quickly moves to talking about principles for success in life and ends the short message with another inspiring story. There is a closing couple of songs with strobe lights and emotionally uplifting songs. The pastor invites anyone who wants to come to the altar, where you can "receive Jesus as your personal Lord and Savior and have life more abundantly." At the end of the last song, another pastor comes up to pray and dismisses the service. He cracks a couple of jokes, reminds the people of what is coming and the offering box at the back of the church, and prays. At the end of the service the large crowd leaves. Most are inspired, moved, and even some a little bit emotional. It reminds you of the concerts you grew up going to, with the number of people and the performance you just witnessed. You pick up your kids in an area that resembles Disneyland and are impressed with all the goodies they got. You leave there having done your duty to attend church that day and having "worshipped God." You are amazed at all the people this church is reaching. Thousands all across your region. When any criticism is leveled against their methodology for "reaching" people the leadership points to the fruitfulness of the church and their influence. They respond with the line of thinking, "Well it has to be of God for this great number of people to worship here." They may even say, "Well, people who do not like our church are just jealous of what God has done here. We are not doing anything expressly forbidden in the Scripture. We have not crossed any lines. We have not disobeyed any Scripture. We are engaging our culture and being all things to all people to win them to the Lord Jesus." The large crowds, the celebrity pastor who has many books on the market, the great programs, are all means they believe justify their church formation. You leave this place wowed by the excellence of the praise band and pastor. Astonished and overjoyed at how great of a time your kids had. But you left not really engaging with anyone in a meaningful way. You were a face in a crowd much like a concert venue. That week you get a follow-up card and a thank you for visiting.

The Regulative Church (Spirit and Truth Church)

Spirit and Truth Church is a smaller congregation. This church is not well-known and oftentimes not well liked by much of popular evangelical culture. The only reason you are attending is a friend from work goes here and you just see something amazingly different in his life at work than the rest of your co-workers and even "fellow Christians." You arrive and the people are loving and kind but there is no café or Starbucks coffee bar. The church itself is smaller (upfront, smaller does not always mean healthy nor does big mean unhealthy). This local church feels more "sacred" when you walk in. You notice that everyone there has their Bibles with them and the conversations around you as you prepare to go to service center around the gospel and the doctrines of the faith. The people welcome you and tell you about the nursery and the kids' programs available. They do their best to help you but you notice that most of the kids over a young age are in the sanctuary with their families. That seems like a lot of work to you. The pre-service starts with announcements and a meet and greet. Then the church does something odd in our culture. They open worship service with a call to worship from the reading of a Scripture passage (a lot of times lengthy) and a pastoral prayer of sorts. The song leader then begins to lead the church in worship though the stage and congregational lights are not dimmed nor is there really an overpowering presence on the stage. You notice the congregation sings loudly the rich truths about the doctrines of the Christian faith to the point the song leader's voice is not clearly heard a majority of the time. After a few songs there is another Scripture reading and prayer. This time the prayer is one of confession of sin and assurance of forgiveness in Christ Jesus. Followed by another song, more contemporary in nature, yet rich in doctrine none the less. Next is the offering prayer after the men come forward to take the offering plates. Upon the prayer's ending the offering is collected as the church worships in their giving of their tithes and offerings unto God. The lead pastor comes to the stage after the offering and offertory prayer. The pastor asks everyone to stand out of reverence for the Word of God and reads his passage of Scripture. The church is going through a book of the Bible. They as a faith family go verse by verse, book by book. The pastor reads the passage with all standing and then prays. The church sits down and the pastor for the next forty-five minutes expounds the meaning of the passage in its original context and applies it to the church. There is little humor and much explanation of the scriptural passage being examined. You feel the weight of the holiness of God and the love of this church for the gospel as it is being expounded from the Word. As the sermon comes to an end the pastor prays and the church then sings a song of response. No special call to the "altar." Just a song of reflection that corresponds to the Scripture preached. Lastly, another pastor whom they call an elder comes up and pronounces a scriptural benediction over the church, then prays once more as the church dismisses. This church, significantly smaller than the other, seems to hunger for the truth and feels like a family. They stay around after the service chatting, smiling, and fellowshipping for a good while. They are not in a hurry to beat the crowd out. They genuinely love being around each other. They do strive to make guests welcome and even invite new guests out to lunch with them. As you leave this service what has been impressed upon your mind and heart is how serious the Bible is to these people and how uncomfortable you felt in the service with all the talk about God and who he is and what Christ has done for sinful man. It was a weighty service and they only had one service where young and old were there together. It was odd to you in contrast with the other service where you left emotionally charged and motivated to be a better version of yourself. You leave feeling a mixture of things from this church. You never heard the depths of your own unworthiness before God before and that was not comfortable for you. You thought God existed to make you happy and here you heard that you exist for his glory. A glory that sets a standard you fall infinitely short of. You need a Savior to take your penalty for sin. You are perplexed. After all, you have asked Jesus into your heart before at a service like the one from Relevant Church and are living a great life filled with many material blessings. God is blessing you, right? In this service you get the sense that, if you faced the God this church read about and preached, you would be cast away to forever face his wrath in hell. You begin to see that the Lord Jesus is not ultimately about making you happy as he is about making you holy, set apart and forgiven through his substitutionary death on the cross in your place. The weight of these things causes you lack of sleep and distress. The weight of what was read, sung, and preached is pressing on your heart heavily.

Which Church was Pleasing to God?

Which church was pleasing to God? Relevant Church (the normative church) or Spirit and Truth Church (the regulative church)? If you would pick up any modern evangelical magazine the normative church, Relevant Church, would be the church on the front cover expounding its great influence and work for the kingdom of God. It would be the church being shown as the church that is most pleasing God in its innovative relevance with its great missiological contextualization. But is that perception correct? Do the ends of large crowds justify the means? The normative church is working by a lot of measurable statistics. They are leading the region in baptisms. They are ministering to thousands. They have millions of dollars to use for their efforts and programs. They are doing great things to help marginalization and poverty. They have the finest buildings and the most creative staff anywhere in the "church world." They are the epitome of pragmatism, which is the philosophy that: if it works, it must be right. Whatever works! They don't really divide on doctrine and they do claim to be fluid on many things. Which church is pleasing to God? To answer that question let us look at two churches in a section of Scripture where the Lord Jesus addressed the seven churches in Asia personally (Rev 2–3). In Rev 2–3 the Lord Jesus addresses seven churches in modern-day Turkey to personally convey to them what they are doing well and not so well. We are particularly going to look at the first two churches addressed in Rev 3 of the seven that the Lord Jesus addresses.

Sardis

The first church the Lord Jesus addresses in Rev 3 (which is actually the fifth church he addresses of the seven) is Sardis in Rev 3:1–6. The Lord Jesus states this to the church in Sardis in Rev 3:1, "To the angel of the church in Sardis write: He who has the seven Spirits of God and the seven stars, says this: '*I know your deeds, that you have a name that you are alive, but you are dead*'" (emphasis mine). The Lord Jesus knows this church from eternity past. He states to them that they "have a name that you are alive, but you are dead." They are a church whose reputation amongst the other churches is great. They are seen by all the other churches to be successful and influential. If a well-read evangelical magazine had been published in that time, they would have been the church on the front cover. Yet in the Lord Jesus' eyes they are dead, filled to the brim with unconverted goats and just a few true sheep. They are the normative church that everyone is applauding but the Lord Jesus states about them later in this text, "*So remember what you have received and heard; and keep it, and repent. Therefore, if you do not wake up, I will come like a thief, and you will not know at what hour I will come to you. But you have a few people in Sardis who have not soiled their garments; and they will walk with Me in white, for they are worthy*" (Rev 3:3-4, emphasis mine). Only few had not compromised the gospel and the Word of God. Only a few were truly of Jesus. This large influential church was filled primarily with people who would die and wake up in hell because they were unconverted goats. Only a few sheep amongst this great membership. They were culturally relevant it appears yet eternally a failure. They had soiled their garments per the Lord Jesus' own words. In their view likely they did not see anything wrong with bringing the world into the church. They were just being relevant. All things to all people! Yet in viewing the commands of God as boundaries not to be crossed instead of truth to govern all their life, both personally and corporately they had soiled their garments. Jesus called them come alive. To wake up or he was going to come in judgment. In the professing Christian world's eyes, they were successful, making a huge difference for the kingdom of God. In Jesus' eyes they were dead and eternally insignificant. They are the normative church.

Philadelphia

The next church is Philadelphia from Rev 3:7-13. The Lord Jesus states to them in Rev 3:8, "*I know your deeds. Behold, I have put before you an open door which no one can shut, because you have a little power, and have kept My word, and have not denied My name*" (emphasis mine). He tells them that he eternally knows who they are. Jesus eternally knows this people. He knows what defines their lives. Their deeds convey the genuineness of their faith. He says they have "little power," conveying their size is likely small and their visible influence as well. They are a small church. Little visible influence in Philadelphia, the city of brotherly love. However, that is not ultimately what really matters to him. He follows that up with a great and glorious commendation that this church has "kept My word, and have not denied My name." The Lord Jesus had nothing negative to say about this small-in-size but great-in-faithfulness church. They were faithful to worship him and live per his Word and for his name as a church. He commends them in the greatest way of all the seven churches in Asia. This is the premier church from the Lord Jesus' perspective. This is the one on his front cover, but is the one the others think is not noteworthy. They are not abundantly wealthy or big in size so they must not be the blessed of the Lord, right? Wrong! This church is commended by the Lord Jesus as faithful and told that he has opened a door for them to victory in his eternal kingdom (Rev 3:9-13). They are a church governed by his Word, doing all they do for his name. They are a regulative church and our Lord Jesus commends them as a faithful, successful church.

Which Church?

Now let us return to our question. Which church is the right model? Which modern church in the tale of the two churches (Relevant Church—normative—versus Spirit and Truth Church—regulative) per the record of Scripture is the successful one? The one that compromises with culture or the one that is faithful in everything to the Word of God and the name of Jesus? The answer is obvious when we look through the lens of Rev 3:1-13. It is the regulative church. Our Lord Jesus does not give us the option on how to serve and worship him. We worship him per his dictates, per his Word. He is the owner of the church. The head of the church. Col 1:18 states, *"He is also head of the body, the church; and He is the beginning, the firstborn from the dead, so that He Himself will come to have first place in everything"* (emphasis mine). If Jesus is the owner of the church then it is his commands that govern both our corporate life and our personal lives. The Lord Jesus Christ is the head of the church, and we are the body. The church, being his body, operates per the directives the head gives. What he tells the body to do it is to do and it is governed by him and his commands. A Christian and a church, to worship God rightly, must worship him per his Word. There really is no other option.

Wait a Minute—
Paul Says "All Things to All People," Right?

Wait a minute. Usually when I hear that, a disagreement is about to start. The idea is: let us not move on yet. I want to discuss this further from a different perspective. One of the greatest arguments (wait a minute) that people make for this idea of incorporating worldly practices into our lives as Christians, both corporately and individually, is Paul's statement in 1 Cor 10:19–23. A lot of evangelicals attempt to be relevant to the fallen world by being like the fallen world with the stated intention of reaching the world for Christ. The problem with that is *what you win them with, you win them to*. Christian liberty is not, "I'm saved to sin," but rather, "I'm saved to enjoy God and proclaim his excellencies" (Rom 6). Christianity was never meant to be cool, hip, trendy, etc. We follow a Savior who had 120 followers after his ascension, who was rejected by thousands that heard him preach the most wonderous expositions of the Word of God ever uttered. We follow a Savior who told people to deny themselves and carry their cross. The Lord Jesus was in no way hip, but he was and is and will always be relevant. He is the way, the truth, and the life. People today justify living in a way that contradicts God's Word and commands by Paul's statement in 1 Cor 9:19–23, where Paul states:

> *For though I am free from all men, I have made myself a slave to all, so that I may win more. To the Jews I became as a Jew, so that I might win Jews; to those who are under the Law, as under the Law though not being myself under the Law, so that I might win those who are under the Law; to those who are without law, as without law, though not being without the law of God but under the law of Christ, so that I might win those who are without law. To the weak I became weak, that I might win the weak; I have become all things to all men, so that I may by all means save some. I do all things for the sake of the gospel, so that I may become a fellow partaker of it.*[5]

---

5. Emphasis mine.

Many use this text to justify that it is okay to do what the culture does in order to reach the culture. They do not get what Paul is saying here. In v. 21 Paul makes sure they understand that though he embraces aspects of the culture of the people whom he is trying to reach, he is first under the law of Christ and will not take on a practice that is against the law of God, particularly the law of the Lord Jesus. Paul states that he is under the law of Christ in v. 21. "Under" conveys being governed by and regulated by. Paul's whole motive is not to be culurally relevant, which is a common Christian buzzword today. Rather his motive is to do all things for the gospel, which is timeless and always relevant. Paul stated in v. 23 of 1 Cor 9, "*I do all things for the sake of the gospel, so that I may become a fellow partaker of it*" (emphasis mine). Paul wanted to remove cultural barriers prohibiting a clear hearing of the gospel so that the gospel would gain a hearing with both Jew and Gentile. He, as one governed and regulated by the law of Christ, removed things from his life that would erect a barrier to the hearing of the gospel.

Paul desired to remove anything that was distracting his audience's attention from hearing and understanding the gospel. Let me illustrate the principle like this. Let us pretend you have a dinner meeting to attend. It is at a restaurant that requires business casual attire with a group of investors who will also be dressed in business casual attire. You get off work, prepare your presentation, excited to share the wondrous news you have to the group of investors, and you put on your jean shorts, favorite Hawaiian shirt, and ball cap. You leave for the restaurant excited about the possibility of them hearing and heeding your presentation. You get there and everyone is staring at you. The investors are already at the table waiting for you to come. They got there a little early. You approach them and the smiles on their faces quickly change as they look at your outfit. You sit down and begin to talk, but notice they really are not engaging in the conversation. You ask if it is okay to start the presentation and several of them make a quick statement that something has come up and they leave. The few that remain get up from the table, come over, and state, "You really should have thought more about this." Now it's easy to look at that restaurant and that meeting group as snobbish and smug. However, we cannot expect the unsaved to act saved, can we? You cannot expect people to share your preferences. And the reality is your poor choice to not dress appropriately prevented your life-changing presentation from even being heard. It would not have been wrong to dress in business casual. Being governed by the law of Christ did not prevent you from wearing business casual; rather, it promotes loving your neighbor as yourself, which in this case you failed to do by not limiting your liberty and putting on a business casual outfit. To come prepared in order to remove a stumbling block to hearing the message. Sure, it would not have been who you are in your preferences, but it would have given the life-changing message you love a hearing with an audience who would have greatly benefited from it. Paul is telling the Corinthians in 1 Cor 9:19–23 that his mindset is to be mindful of things which will create a barrier to people hearing the gospel of God all while being governed by the law of Christ to love God and our neighbor. He is not changing how to worship God, approach God, or changing the gospel, which is clear when he says in 1 Cor 9:21 that he is "under the Law of Christ." He is being sensitive to ensure that on his part he does not do anything that will hinder a hearing for the gospel as long as it is under the commands of Christ. Paul would not partake in sexual sin to gain a hearing as that would contradict the very message he would proclaim. But he would have dressed in business casual to gain a hearing which he would have seen as fulfilling the law of Christ by putting another's needs and preferences above his own in order that they may hear and know Jesus.

Maybe another illustration will help us glean the truth of what Paul is saying. Have you ever had a conversation with someone who had a huge chunk of food in their teeth? It is extremely distracting. They can be telling you all sorts of stuff, yet all you can focus on is the food lodged in their teeth. Yet you are being polite and do not tell them as they go on and on. The whole conversation never registers in your mind because you cannot quit staring at the chunk of food in their teeth. However, if they removed the chunk of food lodged in their teeth, then you could focus on what they are saying. Biblical contextualization is removing the food lodged in our teeth in order to give the gospel a clear hearing. We strive to remove the barriers that prevent a hearing of the gospel. Paul is saying he will remove any barrier he can in line with God's Word that prevents an accurate hearing of the gospel with another culture. He does not change the gospel in any way. He does not live in a way that is in contrast to God's commands and attributes. He is under the law of Christ. He worships God per God's dictates in his law. He is just aware of things that may prevent a hearing to the gospel and seeks to remove any distraction he can to hearing the gospel. A life that is not being lived regulated by the commands of Christ is a life that is not attributing to God the praise and honor due to his name. God calls us to ascribe to him honor and glory in our lives being conformed by his grace to his Word both in our individual daily lives as well as our life in the local church. God is offended by worship divorced from his Word. He does not receive it. He stands resolutely against it.

Why is Wrong Worship Offensive to God?

Before we move on to Old Testament (chapter 2) and New Testament examples (chapter 3) that expounds on how God feels concerning worship not governed by his Word, permit me to give one more illustration regarding the importance of worshipping God for who he has revealed himself to be. Please allow me to explain why this is offensive to God. Imagine with me a scenario. A man and women have been married for twenty years. The man hates steak. He is more of a seafood and sushi kind of guy. Well, his wife chooses to rent out the whole back section of their local steakhouse to celebrate with their friends and family their twenty years of marriage. The wife has prepared a poem to read to her husband in front of her friends and family. The night arrives. They go to the dinner, much to the husband's frustration in finding out it is a steak restaurant. On the way he expresses his disappointment because he told his wife for years now that he does not like steak and yet she has ignored it. The wife, unknown to the husband, also has prepared a poem in his honor that she is going to surprise him with and read. They arrive greeted by friends and family and have their meal, a meal he hated. At the end of the evening the wife stands up to read her poem. In the poem she outlines her love's beautiful brown eyes, dark curly hair, and broad shoulders. She outlines how much she loves his humor and introverted personality. As she reads the poem her husband is visibly upset, the guests stunned, and the whole atmosphere tense. Why? Her husband has blue eyes, blonde hair, and a slender frame. He is not funny at all and yet is a people person. The reason the husband is angry is it becomes clear that the man in the poem is not him. Either this a terrible joke, she clearly does not see her husband for who he is, or she has a lover on the side in idolatry. Either way he is offended and disrespected. He is disrespected in how his wife ignored his statements concerning his dislike of steak. He is angry that his wife read a poem that did not describe him rightly at all. *Imagine how the Lord Jesus and all the triune God responds when his bride ignores his statements, says things, sings things, and does things that are not in line with his attributes and who he is as expressed in his Word.* Chapters 2–3 show us exactly how God feels when he is worshipped not per his commands and not seen rightly by his people. Let us explore the two testaments with the same message.

Discussion Questions

1. What is worship?
2. What is the regulative principle of worship?
3. Why is biblical worship important to examine and understand?

2

Two Testaments, Same Message—Old

DEUT 12:32

Whatever I command you, you shall be careful to do; you shall not add to nor take away from it.[6]

The Old Testament Covenant Aimed at Producing Worshippers of God Governed by Commands of God

MOSES TOLD ISRAEL ON behalf of Yahweh God, that "whatever [meaning everything given by God in the Mosaic covenant] I command you, you shall be careful to do" (Deut 12:32a). God made it clear in the Old Testament that his people were to be "careful" to do everything that he (God) had said. They were to be governed not just by the laws they found helpful in their preferences but they were to carefully submit out of faith in God's promises to all of God's law in order to worship him rightly. The message, with regards to worship in the Old Testament, was that we can only ascribe to God glory and honor per careful observance of his Word.

How does God feel when his people violate his Word and worship him their way? Occasionally in the Old Testament, God would break out against his people to remind them that he is holy and he must be worshipped per *all* the instructions in his Word.

Only as Israel ordered their personal lives and national identity by God's law would their ascribing to him honor and praise be right and good. God demands that we worship him governed by his Word. In this chapter we will look at three examples where God breaks out in judgment to remind his people of that reality and in these examples get a clear picture of how God feels regarding worship that is not governed by his given Word.

Two Testaments, Same Message — Old

Example 1: The Golden Calf in the Room

Exod 32:1–10

Now when the people saw that Moses delayed to come down from the mountain, the people assembled about Aaron and said to him, "Come, make us a god who will go before us; as for this Moses, the man who brought us up from the land of Egypt, we do not know what has become of him." Aaron said to them, "Tear off the gold rings which are in the ears of your wives, your sons, and your daughters, and bring *them* to me." Then all the people tore off the gold rings which were in their ears and brought *them* to Aaron. He took *this* from their hand, and fashioned it with a graving tool and made it into a molten calf; and they said, "This is your god, O Israel, who brought you up from the land of Egypt." Now when Aaron saw *this*, he built an altar before it; and Aaron made a proclamation and said, "Tomorrow *shall be* a feast to the Lord." So the next day they rose early and offered burnt offerings, and brought peace offerings; and the people sat down to eat and to drink, and rose up to play.

Then the Lord spoke to Moses, "Go down at once, for your people, whom you brought up from the land of Egypt, have corrupted *themselves*. They have quickly turned aside from the way which I commanded them. They have made for themselves a molten calf, and have worshiped it and have sacrificed to it and said, 'This is your god, O Israel, who brought you up from the land of Egypt!'" The Lord said to Moses, "I have seen this people, and behold, they are an obstinate people. Now then let Me alone, that My anger may burn against them and that I may destroy them; and I will make of you a great nation."[7]

---

7. Emphases mine.

True Worship

Have you ever heard the phrase "the elephant in the room"? The idea is that there is a source of tension or an unspoken underlying issue that was not addressed or being addressed. For many Christians who have family and friends that are unbelievers, their love for Jesus is the elephant in the room at family get-togethers or friends gatherings. In Exod 32:1–10, as Moses is on the mountaintop, there is not an elephant in the room of Israel's worship of God; rather, there is a golden calf. This golden calf is going to be the source of great tension between God and his people. What is interesting about this account is how Israel viewed the golden calf formed by Aaron. I have heard many people in perplexity of this account say "why would they forsake Yahweh so soon for a false god?" However, there is an important underlying ideology we need to understand. Israel did not see themselves as forsaking Yawheh God. Rather they saw themselves as worshipping Yahweh God yet through means familiar to them from their exile. In v. 5 of Exod 32 they declare a feast to the LORD (LORD being the translation of the Hebrew "Yahweh," which is God's proper name per Exod 3). They see worshipping Yahweh God through the image of a golden calf (calf likely representing strength) as okay. However, God had explicitly told them in Exod 20:4–5:

> "You shall not make for yourself an idol, or any likeness of what is in heaven above or on the earth beneath or in the water under the earth. You shall not worship them or serve them; for I, the LORD your God, am a jealous God, visiting the iniquity of the fathers on the children, on the third and the fourth generations of those who hate Me, but showing lovingkindness to thousands, to those who love Me and keep My commandments."

And in Exod 20:22–23:

> Then the LORD said to Moses, "Thus you shall say to the sons of Israel, 'You yourselves have seen that I have spoken to you from heaven. You shall not make *other gods* besides Me; gods of silver or gods of gold, you shall not make for yourselves.[8]

---

8. Emphasis mine.

God told the people that they were not to make idols. The golden calf was an idol. He told them he spoke to them from heaven showing that he could not be represented through any visible thing in their worship because he is high above his creation. He is Spirit. To worship him through an image of any sort was to demean his nature and dishonor his majesty. The people, still plagued with poor practices from Egypt and the influence of pagan worship on their worldviews, did not heed God's clear instructions concerning worshipping him. When Moses, their representative from God, remained away for many days on the mountain, they despaired and desired to go to God through an idol which would represent God to them. They forsook the commands of God and worshipped God their own way. The response was that God sent Moses back down the mountain. Moses, upon seeing them worship God through this idol, in anger threw down the Ten Commandments smashing them to pieces, and bringing forth God's judgment to the people. Moses confronts Aaron concerning the people's mistake and Aaron shifts the blame to the people. He, Aaron, states in v. 22, *"Do not let the anger of my lord burn; you know the people yourself, that they are prone to evil"* (emphasis mine). Aaron's response was: "I gave the people, who are evil, what they wanted." Aaron here was a poor pastor. He gave the people what they wanted instead of what God had commanded them to do. The result was judgment. Per Exod 32:28, three thousand people fell in judgment to the sword that day. Later in Exod 32:35, we read, *"Then the LORD smote the people, because of what they did with the calf which Aaron had made"* (emphasis mine). God's judgment was swift. Why?

The people of God at the foundation of the Mosaic covenant, where God was forming them as a theocracy, had to understand that God is their King and they are to worship and serve their King per his commands. He owns his people. He redeemed them from slavery in Egypt with a strong hand and glorious might. He saved them to know him and to worship him rightly. They were reminded that worship and service not governed by the Word of God (regulative principle) is not genuine worship unto God at all. Shortly after this account Aaron's own sons would fall into a similar error as Israel did here.

Example 2: Strange Fire

Lev 10:1–3

> Now Nadab and Abihu, the sons of Aaron, took their respective firepans, and after putting fire in them, placed incense on it and offered strange fire before the Lord, which He had not commanded them. And fire came out from the presence of the Lord and consumed them, and they died before the Lord. Then Moses said to Aaron, "It is what the Lord spoke, saying,
> 'By those who come near Me I will be treated as holy,
> And before all the people I will be honored.'"
> So Aaron, therefore, kept silent.

Strange fire! It was just a slightly different mixture of incense. Not that big of a deal, right? Surely God would not care if a variation of the incense offered on the golden altar was different. Perhaps this composition was more economical or more soothing to the senses. Regardless of motive, as we are not told in the account, God responds strongly. In Lev 10:1–3 we once again get a picture of God's response to worship that is in variance with his clear instructions. God had told Moses on Mt. Sinai in Exod 34:34–37:

> Then the Lord said to Moses, "Take for yourself spices, stacte and onycha and galbanum, spices with pure frankincense; there shall be an equal part of each. With it you shall make incense, a perfume, the work of a perfumer, salted, pure, *and* holy. You shall beat some of it very fine, and put part of it before the testimony in the tent of meeting where I will meet with you; it shall be most holy to you. The incense which you shall make, you shall not make in the same proportions for yourselves; it shall be holy to you for the Lord."[9]

God expected Aaron's sons, who represented the people of God unto God, to do their function as priests per his exact commands. To lead the people of God in the worship of God, governed by the law of God given to them. When Moses was on Mt. Sinai before

---

9. Emphasis mine.

this event, God told Moses often *to do exactly* what he was showing Moses on the mountain with regards to the items used for the worship of God in the tabernacle and the tabernacle itself (i.e., Exod 25:9, 40; 26:30; 27:8). God was extremely detailed concerning the daily sacrifices, the setup of the tabernacle, and the role of the Aaronic priesthood. What God expected was that the worship at the tabernacle unto him was to be done per his exact commands. The notion that the people were allowed to do in the worship of God what he had not strictly forbidden was foreign to what he told Moses on the mountain. They were only to do what God commanded in the worship of him. God made that point powerfully when Aaron's two oldest sons offered incense not per the exact makeup God had put forth. In v. 2 fire came out of the LORD's presence and consumed Aaron's sons. God's reasoning expounded to Aaron through Moses was, "*By those who come near to Me I will be treated as holy, And before all people I will be honored*" (v. 3, emphasis mine). Aaron kept silent and was not allowed to mourn the death of his two oldest sons. What is the point?

We as human beings can be forgetful. We forget instructions, the importance of certain lessons learned in times past, and even important dates. How many of us have went to the store and forgotten to pick up items we were instructed to get? Or forgotten birthdays or perhaps anniversaries? God breaks out here in righteous and perfect judgment to remind Aaron and all the people that he is holy and will only be worshipped exactly per his commands, precepts, and instructions. God breaks out against Aaron's sons to remind all God's people that the worship of God is regulated by God's Word. The sons of Aaron approached God their own way (normatively) and the response was judgment. God did not want Aaron or any descendant after Aaron to ever forget: God is holy and those who minister before God will treat him as holy. God would later remind the man, who God called a man after his own heart in 1 Sam 13:14, this same truth.

Example 3: Unholy Hands

2 Sam 6:1–8

Now David again gathered all the chosen men of Israel, thirty thousand. And David arose and went with all the people who were with him to Baale-judah, to bring up from there the ark of God which is called by the Name, the very name of the LORD of hosts who is enthroned *above* the cherubim. They placed the ark of God on a new cart that they might bring it from the house of Abinadab which was on the hill; and Uzzah and Ahio, the sons of Abinadab, were leading the new cart. So they brought it with the ark of God from the house of Abinadab, which was on the hill; and Ahio was walking ahead of the ark. Meanwhile, David and all the house of Israel were celebrating before the LORD with all kinds of *instruments made of* fir wood, and with lyres, harps, tambourines, castanets and cymbals.

But when they came to the threshing floor of Nacon, Uzzah reached out toward the ark of God and took hold of it, for the oxen nearly upset *it*. And the anger of the LORD burned against Uzzah, and God struck him down there for his irreverence; and he died there by the ark of God. David became angry because of the LORD's outburst against Uzzah, and that place is called Perez-uzzah to this day.[10]

What is more acceptable to God? Dirt or the human hand? The account of 2 Sam 6 is a strong statement whereby God declares the human hand is contaminated with sin and cannot approach the throne of God apart from atonement of sin. The backstory of this great account is the end of the period of judges in Israel's history. The ark of the covenant had been captured by the Philistines, who defeated Israel and destroyed the sons of the high priest, Eli (1 Sam 1–5). Later the ark of the covenant was returned by the Philistines on an oxcart after God had crushed them with tumors (1 Sam 5–6). The ark was eventually taken to the house of Abinadab,

---

10. Emphasis mine.

who was entrusted with its care until David came to bring the ark into Jerusalem after he, David, becomes king over all Israel (2 Sam 6). The ark as well as the tabernacle were to be handled a certain way as well as by a certain family line from the tribe of Levi. Per Num 4:5–15 the Kohathites of the tribe of Levi were to carry the ark, and other items in the tabernacle, using the poles attached to the ark after the priests had covered it. In Num 4:17–20 we see an interesting statement made:

> Then the LORD spoke to Moses and to Aaron, saying, "Do not let the tribe of the families of the Kohathites be cut off from among the Levites. *But do this to them that they may live and not die when they approach the most holy objects*: Aaron and his sons shall go in and assign each of them to his work and to his load; but they shall not go in to see the holy objects even for a moment, or they will die."[11]

The Kohathites who were to carry the ark covered were not to look on it uncovered or they would die. In 2 Sam 6 we see David take a pragmatic approach to the worship of God. The ark had been in the house of Abinadab and God had blessed the house of Abinadab greatly. David likely would have been told of how the Philistines had put the ark on an ox cart to transport it and it seemed to work for them. Therefore, David must have reasoned that if it worked it must be right. The ark was put on an ox cart and shuttled towards Jerusalem. Providentially the ark started to come off the ox cart and Uzzah, with zeal for God, reached out to steady it. His hand touched the ark and his life was required of him (2 Sam 6:6–7). In 2 Sam 6:7 God's anger burned against Uzzah. Uzzah was just doing *what he thought was right*. The problem is the whole situation with the ark was wrong. It was in contrast to God's clear commands given through Moses. David learned this lesson after a moment of anger and likely despair. David after this incident put the ark in the house of Obed-edom in 2 Sam 6:10–11. Upon hearing of God blessing the house of Obed-edom David resumed taking the ark to

---

11. Emphasis mine.

Jerusalem, but this time he did in line with the law of God. 2 Sam 6:13–15 records the event:

> And so it was, that when the bearers of the ark of the LORD had gone six paces, he sacrificed an ox and a fatling. And David was dancing before the LORD with all his might, and David was wearing a linen ephod. So David and all the house of Israel were bringing up the ark of the LORD with shouting and the sound of the trumpet.[12]

David on the second attempt had the proper procedures in place and even wore a linen ephod. The ark was carried as it was supposed to be per the Word of God, not shipped pragmatically on an oxcart.

Why did God break out against Uzzah? After all, Uzzah did what he did for the love of God. The reason is clear. Uzzah assumed that his hand was less contaminated than the dust of the earth it was formed from, which does what God commands. Had Uzzah not reached out his hand the ark would have landed in the dirt. However, that dirt, created by God, does what it was created to do. Uzzah's hand like all mankind was an instrument that was incapable in its fallen state of fully doing all that it was created to do for the glory of God. When it rains, the dirt turns to mud. Uzzah like all mankind was a sinner and his hand, representing himself, did not naturally do what God commands. Uzzah and David, for that matter, did not approach the ark per the commands of God for their good and God's glory. God is the object and the consumer of worship and he reminded David as well as all the people that he was not to be worshipped per their pragmatic methods or ways. *Just because something worked for the Philistines did not mean they were to adapt it for their use.* God was to be honored per the instructions he gave in his Word. He reminded them and us today from this historical example that he, the triune God, is holy and is to be treated as such. Ignorance was not an excuse then and is not an excuse today. Worshippers of God worship him per the clear instructions of his holy Word, governed by God's laws and precepts.

---

12. Emphases mine.

Three Examples, One Message

In all three of these examples we see God respond swiftly to the people's attempt to worship him per their own ideas, cultural ways, and opinions. Each attempt was met with a strong reminder that he, the triune God and Creator of all things, is to be worshipped per the precepts and commands in holy Scripture. He in each story is declaring that he alone defines worship of himself, governs worship of himself, and expects the worship of himself to be carried out as instructed. The people of God simply cannot worship God their own way. We cannot do it our own way. As followers of Christ and as local churches we do not have the option of organizing our lives and our gatherings per what has worked for others. We are called to faithfulness. We are called to adoration of the God who alone is great and more beautiful in all his flawless characteristics than any human words can express. We are called to worship him and the only way we, whose hearts are deceitful above all things (Jer 17:9), can worship God is to first know him through Jesus Christ by grace through faith. Then to give him the honor due to his name both individually and as part of the gathering of believers each Lord's day, exactly as he commands us from the inspired, inerrant, and infallible holy Scriptures. To not do so is to make the same mistake as Israel, Aaron's oldest sons, and Uzzah. May we not forget what God said to Aaron in Lev 10:3 "By those who come near Me I will be treated as holy, And before all the people I will be honored." God is in a category all together by himself and he alone is worthy of all worship, honor, and glory. May we ascribe to him worship, honor, and glory as we worship him per his Word!

Discussion Questions

1. What does the golden calf incident teach us about how God is to be worshipped?
2. What was the grave offense of both Aaron's oldest sons and later Uzzah?
3. If God is immutable/unchanging (which he is) then what is the truth about the worship of God that we need to apply to our lives as Christians today?

3

Two Testaments, Same Message—New

MATT 28:16-20

But the eleven disciples proceeded to Galilee, to the mountain which Jesus had designated. When they saw Him, they worshiped Him; but some were doubtful. And Jesus came up and spoke to them, saying, "All authority has been given to Me in heaven and on earth. Go therefore and make disciples of all the nations, baptizing them in the name of the Father and the Son and the Holy Spirit, *teaching them to observe all that I commanded you*; and lo, I am with you always, even to the end of the age."[13]

The Marching Orders of the Church—Produce Worshippers of God Who *Observe All Christ's Commands*

The resurrected Lord Jesus appears to his eleven disciples and gives them the marching orders of the church. He tells them to make disciples (those who are saved by grace through faith in the finished work of the Lord Jesus), to baptize them in the name of the triune God, and then to teach them to "observe all" that Jesus had commanded them. The message of the New Testament with regards to worship is fundamentally the same as the Old Testament.

Sinful man cannot fellowship with God apart from their sin being covered. Jesus' perfect life and earned righteousness, culminating in his death on the cross to pay the penalty for our sin and remove our guilt before God the Father, is the only way we can have a relationship with God as a forgiven people. Jesus himself said in John 14:6b, "*I am the way, and the truth, and the life; no one comes to the Father but through Me*" (emphasis mine). We can only come to God the Father by grace through faith alone in the work of the resurrected and ascended Lord Jesus alone (Eph 2:8–10; Rom 10:9). Once we come to him, we are to learn to "observe" some of what Christ commanded? No! Jesus said in the Great Commission we are to *learn to observe "all" that he commanded*. The word translated "observe" is the Greek word "*tēreō*" and it means to obey, to keep, to guard. We are to learn to guard the commands of God in our hearts and be ruled by them in our lives. The Old and New Testaments are two different covenantal arrangements but the same overall message, especially regarding the worship of God. We can only worship God rightly as his people per his Word.

Many times, with regards to God's discipline of his people in the Old Testament, people will view God's judgment as an Old Testament thing, not a New Testament one. God is immutable, meaning unchanging. He is the same today, yesterday, and will be the same tomorrow. God states in Mal 3:6, "For I, the LORD, do not change; therefore you, O sons of Jacob, are not consumed." God is unchanging and he is perfect in all his unchanging ways. He is perfect in all his attributes. In the time of the Old Testament he interacted with his chosen people through the Mosaic covenantal terms given to them by himself, God, through Moses which looked forward to the coming of the Lord Jesus to fulfill those terms and bring the terms of the new covenant. We looked at three examples in the old-covenant era where God reminded his people of the importance of worshipping him per his Word. In the new covenant God still occasional breaks out against his people, in his loving discipline of them, to remind them of his holiness and that he is to be worshipped by a people who are regulated by his Word. Old and New Testament are two covenants but with the same message with regards to worship of the one true God. In this chapter we will look at three examples from the New Testament of God reminding his people that he is to be worshipped by a people who are regulated and governed by his Word.

Example 1: Holy Anger

MARK 11:15-18

> Then they came to Jerusalem. And He entered the temple and began to drive out those who were buying and selling in the temple, and overturned the tables of the money changers and the seats of those who were selling doves; and He would not permit anyone to carry merchandise through the temple. And He began to teach and say to them, "Is it not written, 'My house shall be called a house of prayer for all the nations'? But you have made it a robbers' den." The chief priests and the scribes heard this, and began seeking how to destroy Him; for they were afraid of Him, for the whole crowd was astonished at His teaching.

Many of us know what it means to be angry. Perhaps even the word itself brings forth a recent memory where you were angry because of something done, said, or not done rightly. Anger in itself is not sin, though much of human anger is rooted in sinful motives. God is angry with sinners. David in Ps 7:11 states, "God is a righteous judge, And a God who has indignation every day." The word indication means "a state of wrath" or "anger" in the original language.[14] God is perfect and cannot sin. He is never out of control and cannot transgress his own moral standards. He is perfect and pure. Therefore, God's anger is not a sin. It is pure and good. The incarnate Son of God's, the Lord Jesus' perfect, sinless, controlled, and righteous anger, is most passionately and powerfully on display when he drives out the merchants and turns over tables in the temple courts. In Mark 11:15–18 we see how Jesus,

---

14. Swanson, *Dictionary of Biblical Languages*.

God the Son, feels with regards to false worship taking place not per God's Word. The Lord Jesus enters the temple court (court of the Gentiles) during his passion week and he drives out all those who are buying and selling in the temple. He overturns the money changers and the seats of those selling doves. The cattlemen and the money changers had set up their business enterprises to serve all the traveling pilgrims in the court of the Gentiles. The animals were sold for the sacrifices as pre-priestly approved sacrifices.[15] The Roman money had to be exchanged for the money used at the temple and extortionately high rates were charged taking advantage of the people.[16] Jesus driving away those selling the animals and the money changers was directly challenging the authority of the high priest.[17] Jesus also would not allow, in v. 16, anyone to casually use the temple grounds as a shortcut, carrying their merchandise, in the city towards the Mount of Olives.[18] By overturning the tables and blocking access to the temple for those who would casually use it, the Lord Jesus was putting on display God's anger at the apostate and false worship happening at the place that was to be where God's people met with God himself to worship him. Jesus quotes Isa 56:7 and Jer 7:11 in Mark 11:17, declaring that the Jews, and particularly their leadership, had made the temple not the place where people came to meet with God but rather where people came to be taken advantage of by thieves. Jesus called what they had made the temple "a den of thieves." This strong statement was our Lord Jesus' way of declaring that the worship of God at the temple had become an apostate mockery of the true God and had procured God's great anger. In 70 AD the temple was destroyed by Titus in God's judgment against Israel, exactly what Jesus predicted would happen in Matt 24:2.

The Lord Jesus' anger here is intensely conveyed in response to the worship of God that was not being governed in all its details by the Word of God. The response of the triune God to normative

---

15. Barker and Kohlenberger III, *Expositor's Bible Commentary*, 180–81.
16. Barker and Kohlenberger III, *Expositor's Bible Commentary*, 180–81.
17. Barker and Kohlenberger III, *Expositor's Bible Commentary*, 180–81.
18. Barker and Kohlenberger III, *Expositor's Bible Commentary*, 180–81.

worship is not indifference. The Lord Jesus manifests the entire triune God's feelings concerning the worship of God's professing people when it is not in line with God's Word or governed by God's Word. There is a holy anger. Jesus particularly was furious that the people, who should have known better from the Word, were treating the worship of the Holy God of glory with little to no reverence or awe. They even went to the point of exploiting those who traveled miles and days to come and worship God.

In our modern time there is a lot of business and marketing that surrounds pastors and Christianity in the Western world. We live in the time of the celebrity pastor and churches whereby many "pastors" will fleece the professing people of God to procure a luxurious lifestyle filled with all the material trappings of this world. Pastors, books, and products are marketed. Many church buildings are a one-stop shop with food courts, gyms, bookstores, etc. I read about one church from an older article that had an arcade, food court, bookstore, sports fields, and even a Starbucks. An attendee of that church stated about the experience, "It's not like, 'Oh, gosh, I have to go to church and be bored and have them spit scripture in my face.' It's like it's fun and they make it great to learn."[19] How does Jesus feel about such a place? It is attracting thousands. It is claiming to have been used of God to reach many people. I'm sure the priests of the Lord Jesus' day could have made similar claims concerning the temple and the commerce in it. Maybe they even justified it with the large numbers coming each year to "worship God." Yet resolutely the Lord Jesus' response was to clear the temple in holy anger against an apostate religion. If the Lord Jesus is unchanging per Heb 13:8, then what would the Lord Jesus' feelings be toward that same root scenario taking place in gatherings that claim to be all about him yet follow none of his precepts and commands? The only logical answer is holy anger. A holy anger rooted in the disobedience of unregenerate professing worshippers of him not being governed and regulated by his Word for his glory. The example of the Lord Jesus in the temple teaches us how the triune God feels towards "worship" divorced from

19. "Mega Churches."

God's Word. As deadly as worldliness is, tradition not rooted in Scripture can be equally as destructive, as we will read about next.

Example 2: Worship God by Tradition?

Matt 15:1–9

> Then some Pharisees and scribes came to Jesus from Jerusalem and said, "Why do Your disciples break the tradition of the elders? For they do not wash their hands when they eat bread." And He answered and said to them, "Why do you yourselves transgress the commandment of God for the sake of your tradition? For God said, 'Honor your father and mother,' and, 'He who speaks evil of father or mother is to be put to death.' But you say, 'Whoever says to *his* father or mother, "Whatever I have that would help you has been given *to God*," he is not to honor his father or his mother.' *And by this you invalidated the word of God for the sake of your tradition.* You hypocrites, rightly did Isaiah prophesy of you:
>
> "This people honors Me with their lips,
> But their heart is far away from Me.
> But in vain do they worship Me,
> Teaching as doctrines the precepts of men."[20]

Many of us have traditions. Family traditions. Work traditions and yes, many churches have traditions they do each year. Traditions are not inherently bad. They form much of the fabric of how people make memories each year and do things with family, faith family, friends, and neighbors. However, there are some traditions that are deadly to the soul and detrimental to the spread of the gospel. In Matt 15:1–9 Jesus is confronted by a group of scribes (lawyers in the Old Testament law) and Pharisees from Jerusalem. They came with an agenda, angry at his refusal to keep their traditions and customs. In v. 2 they state, "Why do your disciples break

---

20. Emphases mine.

the tradition of the elders?" and then they state the tradition the disciples apparently were breaking, "For they do not wash their hands when they eat bread." Per one commentator, "The 'tradition of the elders' refers to the great corpus of oral teaching that commented on the law and interpreted it in detailed rules of conduct, often recording the diverse opinions of competing rabbis. This tradition in Jesus' time was largely oral, but the Pharisees viewed it as having authority very nearly equal to the canon. It was codified about A.D. 135-200 to form the Mishnah."[21] The leaders of Israel saw the traditions of the elders as a fence around the law of Moses to ensure no one broke the law. The strictness of the traditions was meant to guard the law as well as apply the principles of the law to the people. Therefore, the tradition of the elders went further than the law in many matters.

For example, in our text the Pharisees bringing up the "washing of hands." The Old Testament law had no requirement for the Jewish people to wash their hands ceremonially before a meal. The only group required per the law to wash their hands ceremonially was the priests going about their duty in Exod 30:17-21. The Pharisees' traditions took that principle and applied it to all of the Jews, making them wash their hands ceremonially before a meal. Remember the idea of these man-made traditions was a strictness greater than the law to fence the law in and in this case, it was to ensure no one was ceremonially unclean. The Lord Jesus did not heed the "tradition of the elders" commands as he correctly saw through their human traditions as a wicked attempt for sinners to justify themselves through ceremony before a holy God. The Lord Jesus kept all the law of Moses perfectly but did not heed as authoritative the traditions of the elders and commandments of men.

In this account the Lord Jesus responds with a rebuke to these Pharisees and scribes. He picks an example showing the errancy of the tradition of elders. An example where our Lord Jesus expounds how the law of God and the tradition of the elders contradicted one another, therefore they both could not be right. Jesus pointed out in vv. 4-6 that in the tradition of the elders the Jews said it

---

21. Barker and Kohlenberger III, *Expositor's Bible Commentary*, 74.

was okay to not take care of one's parents (a violation of the fifth commandment in Exod 20:12) if they used those funds for "God's work." By their very commands they were saying it is okay to not honor your parents in their need as long as you give those monies/resources to God, thereby disavowing the commandment of God in Exod 20:12 as well as Exod 21:17. The Lord Jesus stated clearly in rebuke that they, the Pharisees, promoted the breaking of the law of God through the commandments of men. The Lord Jesus quoted Isa 29:13 concerning the Old Testament people of God's empty worship of him through man-made commands. He was pronouncing judgment on the Pharisees and scribes as well as the whole canon of the tradition of the elders. From Isaiah 29:13 the Lord Jesus declared that these Pharisees and scribes teach as authoritative man-made commands and that their hearts were far from God just like the audience Isaiah was writing to. The Lord Jesus declared that these religious people were not close to God nor worshipping God rightly or at all. He declared that in their love for man-made traditions and their forsaking of being governed by God's Word alone their worship of God was a farse. The implication of the Lord Jesus' statement is crystal clear. These Pharisees and scribes were not true worshippers of Yahweh God. His rebuke of the Pharisees was a statement of clear judgment against them. The Lord Jesus being the fullest manifestation of the revelation of God (Heb 1:1–3) and God himself (John 1:1, 18) conveys to us here in the New Testament God's hatred for a type of worship that is based on man-made traditions rather than on the Word of God. The Lord Jesus resolutely stood against man-centered traditions, which people abused due to greed, it appears, in order to get out of obeying the clear commands of God. These traditions directly contradicted the inspired, inerrant, and infallible Word of God. The people in that time were either going to be found obeying God's Word or the traditions. They could not in this case and many other cases do both. Today in many churches there are traditions that keep people from rightly worshipping and following God.

Man-made Traditions in the Church?

We have always done it this way! Perhaps you have heard someone state that before. The idea that what they are doing now is something they have always done and it has worked in the past so why change it now. This idea that practice in both personal and corporate worship for Christians is governed by what works is the fruit of a pragmatic mindset. Pragmaticism teaches that if it works, it is right. Much of the traditions that govern God's people in many churches are rooted in pragmaticism and not in the clear commands of Christ Jesus the Lord of glory.

For example, in the region where I pastor many churches still close services with birthdays and anniversaries. The idea is that on a person's birthday or a couple's anniversary they come up and drop some money in a container. Then the whole congregation sings happy birthday to them or an anniversary song for the couple whose anniversary it is. Now it is clear that the Bible tells us and commands us concerning what exactly to do on the Lord's Day gathering. We will look at that in chapter 4 of this book. For now, we can clearly state that everything done in the Lord's Day service or in life in general is to be governed by God's Word if it is to be pleasing to God. That is the consistent theme we see in the examples of the Old and New Testament. The local church worship service itself is to focus on worshipping God. The triune God and his glory is the object of all done in the service. How does singing happy birthday and anniversary songs to people during the service cause God's people to think on the glories of God revealed in Scripture? How does it edify them in the faith? Who is the focus of such a tradition? When you ask people why they do it, the answer is always "that is the way we have always done it," not "we see this in Scripture commanded or an example of this in Scripture." Imagine with me for a moment a pastor preaching on the doctrine of God's justice. It is a heavy message that garnishes much thought from those in the pews. Immediately following the message is a celebration of a birthday in song. The focus moments earlier was on a truth of God from his Word and now has been redirected to person being sung to and celebrated because of a tradition in place. Instead of responding to God's Word with song or a benediction, many churches sing celebration not to God but to a person or persons celebrating the day of their birth or the day of a couple's marriage. The focus per the holy Scripture of our gatherings as God's people is not the celebration of people; rather, it is the celebration of God and his gospel. Traditions, if not rooted in Scripture, can be dangerous and move our focus from the worship of God to the celebration of man.

The Lord Jesus resolutely stood against the Pharisees' and scribes' traditions that annulled the true worship of God by his commands. He pronounced the wrath of God was upon them (the greatest judgment of all). Like the Old Testament, the new covenant brought by our Lord Jesus' perfect substitutionary sacrifice calls for God's redeemed to worship God regulated by his commands. Traditions can be deadly to that end if divorced from God's holy Word.

Example 3: A Sacred Meal

1 Cor 11:23–32

> For I received from the Lord that which I also delivered to you, that the Lord Jesus in the night in which He was betrayed took bread; and when He had given thanks, He broke it and said, "This is My body, which is for you; do this in remembrance of Me." In the same way *He took* the cup also after supper, saying, "This cup is the new covenant in My blood; do this, as often as you drink *it*, in remembrance of Me." For as often as you eat this bread and drink the cup, you proclaim the Lord's death until He comes.
>
> Therefore whoever eats the bread or drinks the cup of the Lord in an unworthy manner, shall be guilty of the body and the blood of the Lord. But a man must examine himself, and in so doing he is to eat of the bread and drink of the cup. For he who eats and drinks, eats

and drinks judgment to himself if he does not judge the body rightly. For this reason many among you are weak and sick, and a number sleep. But if we judged ourselves rightly, we would not be judged. But when we are judged, we are disciplined by the Lord so that we will not be condemned along with the world.[22]

One of the greatest holidays that I look forward to every year is Thanksgiving. The very word "Thanksgiving" elicits the thought of baked turkey, mashed potatoes, green beans, salad, dressing, and the list goes on. My family usually gathers around this meal and, before we eat, uses it as time to convey what we are thankful to God for this past year. It is a time of remembrance and also celebration. For the Christian the greatest meal we meet around in remembrance and celebration is the Lord's Supper. What makes this meal special is that our Lord Jesus told us to do this in remembrance of him (1 Cor 11:24–25). On the night our Lord Jesus was to be betrayed, as the disciples and he celebrated the Passover, Jesus instituted the Lord's Supper, where he took the unleavened bread and said it was his body (v. 24). He took the wine and said this was his blood (v. 25). The deliverance that the Lord Jesus was about to accomplish was going to be a greater deliverance than the first exodus celebrated in the Passover meal. Paul recounts all these things recorded in the Gospels to remind the Corinthians of the clear teaching of Christ concerning what it means to partake in the Lord's Supper table. He reminded the church in Corinth what the Lord Jesus stated with regards to the wine representing his blood and the bread his body. Paul reminds the Corinthians in his epistle to them, inspired by the Holy Spirit, that the Lord Jesus clearly told his people to take of the Lord's Supper as a memorial to reflect on what he accomplished through his body given and blood shed on the cross at calvary.

However, they were not approaching this sacred meal rightly. Rather, they were approaching this meal in disobedience through division. A memorial that signified their coming as one people in Christ was being demeaned by their behavior. Per Paul they were

22. Emphases mine.

divided into cliques and treating the sacred meal as well as each other poorly. Paul told them earlier in 1 Cor 11:20-22, "Therefore when you meet together, it is not to eat the Lord's Supper, for in your eating each one takes his own supper first; and one is hungry and another is drunk. What! Do you not have houses in which to eat and drink? Or do you despise the church of God and shame those who have nothing? What shall I say to you? Shall I praise you? In this I will not praise you." They were a divided bunch not sharing food in their fellowship meal, which was done likely in conjunction with the Lord's Supper. They were divided with one another, neglecting the poor amongst them.

Paul exhorts these Christians in vv. 27-29, "whoever eats the bread or drinks the cup of the Lord in an unworthy manner, shall be guilty of the body and the blood of the Lord. But a man must examine himself, and in so doing he is to eat of the bread and drink of the cup. For he who eats and drinks, eats and drinks judgment to himself if he does not judge the body rightly." He tells them to approach the Lord's Supper after having examined themselves and to not take of the Lord's Supper in an unworthy manner, thereby heaping guilt on themselves. God takes the memorial of his Son's sacrifice to the praise of his name very seriously. Paul urges the Corinthians to do the same. In vv. 30-32, he reminds them that the reason that many of them were sick and some had died was that God disciplined them to remind the church to approach him in the Lord's Supper rightly. Notice what Paul says is God's response to the irreverent taking of the Lord's Supper, "*For this reason many among you are weak* and *sick*, and *a number sleep*. But if we judged ourselves rightly, we would not be judged. But when we are judged, *we are disciplined by the Lord so that we will not be condemned along with the world*" (emphases mine). The point is clear. We cannot approach God in worship lightly. Taking the Lord's Supper is an act of worship. We are celebrating and honoring the person and work of Jesus as we reflect on his body given and blood shed for the remission of his people's sins. We are celebrating him and his work. The Corinthians approached the worship of God in the Lord's Supper ordinance with irreverence and disobedience to

God's command concerning unity (John 13:34–35). The result was God's discipline to remind them of the importance of worshipping him per his Word.

When we strive to approach God in worship loosely, we run the risk of incurring his discipline if we are his people. God will share his glory with no one. God will not allow his name to be demeaned. He reminded Isaiah of that fact. In Isa 55:8 God declared, "I am the Lord, that is My name; I will not give My glory to another, Nor My praise to graven images." God will not share his glory. He will not allow his name to be demeaned. Therefore, we must know God per his Word and approach him in worship per his commands. That is the point underlying Paul's exhortation to the Corinthians. A point we must understand as Christians.

What is the Message of the Two Testaments?

Two Testaments yet the same message! In chapters 2–3 the message concerning ascribing to God honor, praise, and glory due to his name (which is worship) is the same in both the Old and New Testament. The message is this: we can only worship God as we first know God per his holy Word and then approach him in worship governed/regulated by his Word. We cannot attribute honor, praise, and adoration unto God apart from his Word. The Word of God regulates our knowledge of God and our lives lived personally and corporately before him. The question is, will we make the mistakes of many of those in the examples we pondered or will we heed the counsel of Scripture? Will we each be a person and our churches a people whose knowledge of God and worship of God is regulated by God's Word alone?

Discussion Questions

1. Why was Jesus angry with the state of the worship in the temple?
2. What about the Pharisees' approach to God did the Lord Jesus condemn?
3. Why did God bring discipline to the church in Corinth?
4. What is the principle from these examples that we need to apply to our lives and worship of God?

4

True Worship of God in Spirit and Truth

JOHN 3:1-8

Now there was a man of the Pharisees, named Nicodemus, a ruler of the Jews; this man came to Jesus by night and said to Him, "Rabbi, we know that You have come from God as a teacher; for no one can do these signs that You do unless God is with him." *Jesus answered and said to him, "Truly, truly, I say to you, unless one is born again he cannot see the kingdom of God."* Nicodemus said to Him, "How can a man be born when he is old? He cannot enter a second time into his mother's womb and be born, can he?" Jesus answered, "Truly, truly, I say to you, unless one is born of water and the Spirit he cannot enter into the kingdom of God. *That which is born of the flesh is flesh, and that which is born of the Spirit is spirit. Do not be amazed that I said to you, 'You must be born again.' The wind blows where it wishes and you hear the sound of it, but do not know where it comes from and where it is going; so is everyone who is born of the Spirit."*[23]

JOHN 4:21-26

Jesus said to her, "Woman, believe Me, an hour is coming when neither in this mountain nor in Jerusalem will you worship the Father. You worship what you do not know; we worship what we know, for salvation is from the Jews. *But an hour is coming, and now is, when the true worshipers will worship the Father in spirit and truth; for such people the Father seeks to be His worshipers. God is spirit, and those who worship Him must worship in spirit and truth.*" The woman said to Him, "I know that Messiah is coming (He who is called Christ); when that One comes, He will declare all things to us." Jesus said to her, "I who speak to you am *He*."[24]

---

24. Emphases mine.

Worship in Spirit and Truth

Have you ever been to a service that seemed so dead? Dead not in the sense of the liturgy or the reverence of the service, rather the response of the people in the pews/seats. They were lifeless, unexcited to approach God's manifest presence. Likely some reading this have seen that before. We cannot divorce truth from affections. Biblical worship that God calls forth from his people is both truth-based and encompasses all a person is. A person's mind must be engaged in the glory of God. A person's desires must be for the God of glory. A person's will must be freed to enjoy the triune God who alone is worthy of all honor.

Jesus in John 3:1-3 had an encounter with, likely, the most highly regarded teacher of the law in Israel at that time, named Nicodemus. The Lord Jesus met with him at night and despite the pleasant greeting Nicodemus gave Jesus, our Lord Jesus cut right to the heart of Nicodemus' issue. To enter the kingdom of God he had to be born again. In light of Nicodemus' objection Jesus expounds what he meant by being born again. In vv. 6-8 Jesus tells Nicodemus that which is born of the flesh is flesh but that which is born of the Spirit of God is spirit. Then tells him not to be amazed and outlines at the end of v. 8 that being born again means to be born of God the Holy Spirit. The apostle John outlines this account clearly showing that the only way a person will enter the kingdom of God through faith in Jesus is if God the Holy Spirit indwells them and makes their mind, heart, and affections new. Paul stated this truth profoundly in Eph 2:4-5, "But God, being rich in mercy, because of His great love with which he loved us, even when we were dead in our transgressions, made us alive together with Christ (by grace you have been saved)." What is clear is that Paul outlines in detail the doctrine that the apostle John recorded Jesus as stating to Nicodemus. Being born again is to be made new by the Holy Spirit who resides in a person that God has chosen before time to come to know the Lord Jesus (Eph 1:4).

The apostle John puts forth another example where Jesus taught about being born of the Holy Spirit in order to become a child of God. In John 4 the apostle John outlines Jesus' interaction with a Samaritan woman at the well. She engages Jesus in a religious debate after he lovingly points out her sin (she had been married five times). The Lord Jesus responds by telling her a wondrous truth. In John 4:23-24, Jesus states, *"But an hour is coming, and now is, when the true worshipers will worship the Father in spirit and truth; for such people the Father seeks to be His worshipers. God is spirit, and those who worship Him must worship in spirit and truth"* (emphases mine). The Lord Jesus told this woman that God the Father is procuring for himself worshippers in spirit and truth. He then tells her God is spirit and therefore to worship him we must worship him in spirit and truth. What does it mean to worship God in spirit and truth here? If we let the Bible interpret the Bible, then it is clear that John in both stories from John 3-4 means to show his readers that worshipping in spirit and truth is what God produces in all he saves from various backgrounds. A person who is born again, born of the Spirit (John 3:3, 8), is clearly someone whose mind, affections, and will has been renewed to love and grow in loving God instead of inherently be in rebellion to God. Worshipping in truth the apostle John outlines further in John 14:6 when he records the Lord Jesus as saying, "I am the way, and *the truth*, and the life; no one comes to the Father but through Me" (emphasis mine). To worship God in Spirit is to be a person who is born of the Spirit with the result of believing on the person and work of Jesus Christ who is the truth of God. To worship God as a new creature per the fullness of the revelation of God's Word, namely Jesus Christ. One commentator put it this way, "Worship of God can be done only through the One (Jesus) who expresses God's invisible nature and by virtue of the Holy Spirit who opens to a believer the new realm of the kingdom."[25] To worship God rightly can only happen amongst those who are born of the Spirit and worshipping God per his truth which revolves around the Lord Jesus. *The Lord Jesus clearly regulates in John 4:23-24 how God is to be worshipped. He is to be worshipped in spirit and truth.*

---

25. Walvoord and Zuck, *Bible Knowledge Commentary*, 286.

Approaching God our own Way? – Tale of Two Brothers

My brother Jacob and I competed over everything. From putt-putt golf to regular golf to basketball to who was taller. Not only did we compete, but we knew well how to "talk trash." When one of us lost, it was the mission of the other brother to ensure that it was not forgotten in the near future. One of my fondest memories of Jacob is a day at the golf course. He crushed me. From the moment we hit our first shots off the tee till the last putt on the eighteenth green, he had everything going for him. He made sure to secure the score card (I had a tendency to grab them if they were not favorable and accidentally dispose of them with our sodas and chips). The next morning, I remember rolling over in bed and waking up to the score card taped to the ceiling of my room with our scores circled. He wanted me to wake up with the first thing my eyes would gaze on being evidence of my failure and his triumph. That was one of many examples of our competitiveness as brothers. In the first chapter post-fall of Genesis, we see two brothers approach God, one with success and one with failure. It appears that there is almost this sense of competition, though that is a bit of speculation. Both brothers are seeking to be accepted by God and only one walks away with the score card of victory.

In Gen 4 two brothers approach God with a sacrifice. One is rejected. The other accepted. Why did God reject one and accept the other? The answer per the author of Hebrews in Heb 11:4 is that one came to God in faith (Abel), and the other brother (Cain) came to God with the fruit of the work of his hands. Now, in order to have faith there must be an object we have faith in. Therefore, it is clear that what had been revealed by God concerning the worship of himself Abel believed and acted upon, while Cain came in unbelief. Cain approached God not trusting God's revelation of himself and not being governed by it. Abel was received by grace through faith in God's revelation and Cain was rejected in his attempt to worship God his own way. The only way a person can worship God in the church age is in the truth of God as one born of God. All other ways are rejected. Jesus said he was the *only way* to God the Father in John 14:6. True worship, consistent with the Lord Jesus' statement in John 14:6, therefore, cannot be many ways to honor and praise God; rather it is God's ordained way of praising him alone that is received as true worship. Cain worshipped his way and was rejected. Abel came to God per God's Word and was received.

The book of Judges outlines what happens to God's people when they strive to conduct themselves by their own philosophies, opinions, etc. It leads to chaos that mimicked Sodom and Gomorrah (Judg 19–20). The book of Judges ends with the theme of the book, "In those days there was no king in Israel; everyone did what was right in his own eyes" (21:25). A sad diagnosis of Israel's spiritual state. God is holy and will not be worshipped per what is right in man's sight. We must worship him governed (regulated) by his truth as those who are born again, thereby a people whose entire being (mind, will, and emotions) is captured by and moved to honor the triune God who saves his people. What does this look like each day as Christians? What does it look like corporately as a local church? In the rest of this chapter we will examine these two questions. Before we examine those two questions we must first approach the starting line for running the race of worship of God.

The Starting Line to Worship God in Spirit and Truth

To run a race, we must first cross the starting line. To run in a race without ever having registered warrants no reward at the end of the race. Where is the starting line to be a worshipper of God in spirit and truth? It really begins with the Word and knowing how we are to come to God for forgiveness and reconciliation. To be a worshipper of God we must come to God as a sinner who needs the grace of God infinitely more than we can even imagine (Rom 3:23). God is Creator. He is holy and perfect in all his attributes. (All the Psalms outline God's attributes beautifully. See further, Isa 6:1–5.) He is perfectly just and will punish rebels for their rebellion against his cosmic reign. We deserve rightly God's infinite punishment because we have sinned against an infinite God. Since the fall of Adam all of mankind has a sin nature and has inherited Adam's guilt (Rom 5:12-17; Gen 3; etc.). We are spiritually dead (Eph 2:1-3). Our wills are in bondage to sin (Rom 1:18-32). We never seek after God (Rom 3:11-12). We are a people utterly doomed and deprived of anything that would merit God's love and kindness to us. Yet while we were still sinners God sent his Son (Rom 5:8). The Lord Jesus, who is truly God and truly man, born of the virgin Mary lived a perfect/sinless life culminating in his death on the cross in order to be the wrath bearer for God's people in order to cover all our sins before God forever and to impute to us his earned, both active and passive, righteousness (John 1:1-18; 2 Cor 5:21). The Lord Jesus in his death on the cross took the penalty for our sin, removed our guilt, and paid our sin debt before God the Father (Rom 3:21-26; Col 1-2). He declared in victory "it is finished" on the cross and then gave up his Spirit (John 19:30). He was buried in a rich man's tomb and rose from the dead on the third day whereby God the Father validated that the Lord Jesus is indeed God, and his sacrifice on behalf of sinners was accepted before God the Father (Matt 28; Rom 1:4; 1 Cor 15). Jesus ascended forty days later and he and God the Father sent God the Holy Spirit to draw God's foreknown people to himself in Christ (Acts 1-2). Those who turn from sin (repent) and trust in the finished work of the Lord Jesus alone to be saved (biblical faith) are sealed in the Spirit and forever secure as a forgiven sinner and adopted child of God (Eph 1:13-14; Rom 8:23-30; Eph 2:1-10). The only way someone comes to faith in the Lord Jesus is that, as they hear the Word of God and the gospel of grace, God's Spirit resurrects their dead spiritual nature and brings about a new set of desires freed from the bondage of love for sin to now see the glory of Jesus in faith (Rom 10:17; Eph 2:4-10). The starting point of worshipping God truly and rightly is first coming to God through faith in Jesus. Paul outlines it clearly in Col 2:13-14 and Eph 2:8-9, which reads:

> When you were dead in your transgressions and the uncircumcision of your flesh, He made you alive together

> with Him, having forgiven us all our transgressions, having canceled out the certificate of debt consisting of decrees against us, which was hostile to us; and He has taken it out of the way, having nailed it to the cross.
>
> For by grace you have been saved through faith; and that not of yourselves, *it is* the gift of God; not as a result of works, so that no one may boast.[26]

The question I urge you, who are reading this, to ask yourself now is, "am I a Christian? Do I understand the gospel in the terms above?" If so, rejoice and seek to worship God in spirit and truth. If not then I pray by his grace you repent (change your mind about your world-view and life in rebellion against God) and put your faith in the Lord Jesus Christ alone to save you from the penalty due to you for your transgressions and sin before a holy, righteous Creator who you will give an account to. Now that the starting line has been drawn and crossed, let's answer the questions regarding the worship of God daily and corporately for the Christian.

How a Christian Worships God Each Day

Paul outlines in 1 Cor 10:31–11:1 what a born-again Christian's daily focus is to be. Here, he is summarizing a point he is making to the Corinthians concerning Christian liberty (which revolved around how in that time to engage with food sacrifice to idols). Paul told the Corinthians,

> Whether, then, you eat or drink or whatever you do, do all to the glory of God. Give no offense either to Jews or to Greeks or to the church of God; just as I also please all men in all things, not seeking my own profit but the *profit* of the many, so that they may be saved. Be imitators of me, just as I also am of Christ.[27]

He outlined that in everything they did they were to see it as an opportunity to ascribe to God glory and to praise God for his

---

26. Emphasis mine.
27. Emphasis mine.

goodness, grace, and his perfections. This was to lead them into the reality of vv. 32-33, which was a life lived to do others good, especially the church of God so that as many people would come to know and grow in the Lord Jesus. He then tells these Christians to imitate him as he imitates Jesus, who loved God the Father with all his heart, soul, mind, and strength perfectly (Mark 12:30, in which the Lord Jesus quoted from Deut 6:4-5). The Lord Jesus also loved his neighbor as himself perfectly (Mark 12:31, in which the Lord Jesus quoted from Lev 19:18). Jesus did that perfectly. Paul could imitate Jesus on a limited basis, but could not and did not do that perfectly. Nor can we do that perfectly. Regardless we are called to, in the grace of God, imitate Christ and his life pattern of loving God and loving others (which is the Law of Christ expounded in Mark 12:30-31 and really a summary of the commands of Scripture). We are to do all things for the triune God's glory, in whatever we eat or drink (the basics of life). We are governed by the law of Christ, so that all we do is rooted in the love of God and the love for others, especially the church of God. The law of Christ summarizes the intent of all the law and prophets per Jesus in Matt 22:40. Doing all things for the glory of God and good of others is living each day regulated by the law of Christ (Mark 12:30-31; Matt 22:34-40, which was the Lord Jesus' summation of the Ten Commandments and all the Old Testament law).

What does that look like? Remember the law of Christ is to govern all our actions and behaviors. We spend time with the God we love in prayer and in the Word daily (see Jesus' example in Luke 5:16, and his prayer request in John 17:17). We meditate on the truths we learn from the Word. We fast as God leads us in seeking to know him more with our needs (Acts 13:2). We do not steal because we do not want to be stolen from. We do not slander because we do not want to be slandered. We help those in need because we want to be helped when in need. We adore God and love our neighbors as ourselves. Daily we love to live to observe the commands of Christ as baptized disciples of Christ for the glory of Christ.

Paul states in Rom 12:1-2, "Therefore I urge you, brethren, by the mercies of God, to present your bodies a living and holy sacrifice, acceptable to God, *which is* your spiritual service of worship. And do not be conformed to this world, but be transformed by the renewing of your mind, so that you may prove what the will of God is, that which is good and acceptable and perfect" (emphasis mine). Paul stated these things to the Roman church after he had outlined in Rom 1:1-3:20 the doctrine of God as Creator and man as sinner. Then from Rom 3:21-11:36 Paul outlined the doctrine of salvation (election, regeneration, justification, adoption, sanctification, glorification) in detail. From that point, Paul then stated in Rom 12:1, "Therefore I urge you, brethren, by the mercies of God." What are the mercies of God that Paul is urging them with? It is the truth he expounded in Rom 1-11. It is the Christian faith. The reality of the doctrines of the Christian faith is to move the Romans to "present their bodies as a living sacrifice, acceptable to God" and to be "transformed by the renewing of your mind, so that you may prove what the will of God is, that which is good and acceptable and perfect." The doctrines of the faith were to bring forth from God's people lives that would be lived sacrificially before God and minds that would be filled with God's Word. This was to move them to be able to discern God's righteousness and working in the world. In summary, a Christian who worships God in everything is born again by the Spirit of God and their life is governed by the law of Christ, which is the Word of God. They know their Bibles. They seek to live out the commands of Christ not to earn salvation but because they have salvation. Their obedience shows their salvation to be genuine. It does not make them or keep them saved. Their increasing obedience to the commands and repentance from their sin against God is all out of love for Jesus (John 14:15).

A Daily Contradiction For Many "Evangelicals"

Herein lies the problem for much of evangelicalism today. Most of modern evangelicalism claims to believe in the sufficiency of

Scripture but fails to practice what they claim to believe. Many people equate following and worshipping God with being "led by the Spirit." What they mean by that is they feel God's Spirit is revealing God to them apart from his Word. They believe God is giving them dreams, visions, promptings, signs, messages, words, etc. to lead them. Most, not all, in this camp know very little of their Bible, so they are not able to discern these things rightly (1 John 4:1–21). The only way to discern if something is from God is to check it with the Word of God, which we know is the Holy-Spirit-inspired Word of God without any mixture of error (2 Tim 3:16). Most of those who claim to be "Spirit-led" say, do, and think things that are in contradiction to the Word of God rightly divided. They justify it as valid by saying the Spirit of God told them or led them to do this, therefore, "Who are you to argue against God?" Either the Word of God is wrong or they are mistaken concerning what it means to be led by the Spirit of God. Being led by the Spirit of God is to be driven to know God from his Word and out of love for him to obey him per his Word. Being "Spirit-led" is the same as being "Word driven and saturated." Jesus made it clear in his high priestly prayer in John 17 that his people would be sanctified by the truth and he says of the truth, "Your Word is truth" (John 17:17). The Spirit of God cannot be divorced from the truth of God. To worship God daily as a Christian we must be filled with his Spirit and his Word. We must be new creatures born of the Holy Spirit who grow in our knowledge and love of God from his Word to the end that our lives are ordered per the commands of God from the Word of God.

Spirit-Led?

I remember hearing the news that a married couple we were friends with were getting divorced. The wife had come to her pastor and told him that God's Spirit was telling her to leave her husband and go to this other man. She was convinced that she was following the lead of God. The problem is that there was no basis for biblical divorce, nor was she remotely considering what the Spirit of God had inspired in the Word pertaining to this subject. God's inspired Word states in Matt 19:9, "And I say to you, whoever divorces his wife, except for immorality, and marries another woman commits adultery." Per Jesus' own words, inspired by the Spirit and recorded by Matthew, she was definitely not following God's leading. Now while that is an obvious example there are more subtle examples and just as dangerous in many ways. Many people look for signs and wonders (which Jesus calls evil in Matt 16:4). Or they believe that God is telling them to do something, say something, or leave something without little knowledge of God's attributes and commands from his Word. They elevate their experiences to the place of divine truth and devalue the rigorous study of the Word to the realm of theologians. In doing so they claim to be daily led by the Spirit of God, but are just following the dictates of their hearts which we are shown are not trustworthy in Jer 17:9. The Holy Spirit leads us to daily ascribe to God honor through our growth in our knowledge of God's Word, our love for the God of the Word, and our desire to obey the commands of God seen in his Word. A person that worships God daily in true worship is a person that seeks to live per the commands of God, not for salvation, but because the Spirit now lives in them and is giving them the desire to know, love, and follow God in all things. And we will fail at this, though God will faithfully keep us in the faith till the end (1 John 1:8–10; John 10:21–30). We will stumble forward. We will run the race of faith. We will desire to love God more, sin less, and love others more sacrificially. We will want these things especially as we see the Lamb of God's glory from the Word.

Be Encouraged, You Will Struggle

Be encouraged. You will fail. For some that may be more of a discouragement. For others it helps us to realize our daily need for Jesus and our desire for his grace to sanctify us. Let us not forget that there will be battles in our minds and hearts per Gal 5:13–26 and Rom 6–7. However, God's Spirit, through God's word, will lead us in ongoing repentance, faith, and increasing obedience to the law of Christ each day in the joy of the gospel (1 John). We worship God in spirit and truth by trusting in Jesus for salvation alone and following his Word alone by the power of his Spirit alone. Now as an individual Christian we are called to worship God not only daily but also to gather with God's people as a member of a local New Testament church (Heb 10:24–25). To worship God rightly as an individual we must be a part of a weekly gathering of God's people because it is part of his commands for his people. How does the corporate gathering of God's people worship him rightly in spirit and truth?

Worship in Spirit and Truth for the Local Church

What does true worship look like as a group of born-of-the-Holy-Spirit Christians who gather together weekly (a local church)? We are to be a people who worship God in spirit (born again) and truth (adherence to God's Word). The local church is to be a collection of people from various backgrounds, different age groups, even contrasting preferences, who come together each Lord's Day (Sunday) to worship God in spirit and truth. In order to be a people who worship him in spirit, it is only logical that the local church's membership has to be born again (John 3:3) and publicly identified as such through baptism (Acts 2:41). We have outlined that worshipping God in spirit is being born of the Spirit. Being born again. Worshipping God in truth as a local church is conducting ourselves as a local church per his instructions in the Word. Governed in our formation and services by his Word. Regulated by his Word. At this point, before we look at what that looks like in the life of a local church, it is helpful to clearly define what the church is in the New Testament.

The Bible never describes the church as an address or a location. The Bible describes the church with the Greek word "ekklēsia," which at its basic level means "a congregation, an assembly." The word is used in four ways throughout the New Testament. The word is used to describe a local group of born-again (Holy-Spirit-indwelled) Christians who believe on the Lord Jesus, are baptized in Christ, under the care of qualified elders, and who meet weekly around the Word and the sacraments in order to grow in knowledge and grace together (Rom 16:5; Col 4:15). The word "ekklēsia" also describes Christians from all time and all ages, meaning the redeemed of God bought by Christ from every era (Eph 5:23, 25, 27, 29; Heb 12:23). "Ekklēsia" is also used to depict Christians made up of many churches in a particular city during the time of the New Testament (Acts 13:1 ;1 Cor 1:2; Acts 8:1; Rev 2:1). Lastly, "ekklēsia" is also used to describe the redeemed of the Lord Jesus living in that time period (1 Cor 15:9; Gal 1:13; Matt 16:18). From all these examples the basic definition of "ekklēsia" is the congregation of the redeemed of God in Christ Jesus. The church is the people of God. The church is not a place, not a location, not an organization or a religious institution. It is the people of God redeemed by the Lord Jesus Christ. God the Son in his humanity died to purchase a people from every tribe, tongue, and nation.

What is amazing is the Lord Jesus accomplishes his mission of building his church through his church. Now if the church is what Christ died for to the glory of his Father during his first coming, then we should not treat lightly how we organize ourselves in the local church. If Jesus is building the church, do you think it is important to structure each local "ekklēsia" ("church") per his commands or our preferences? Let us put it this way, if the church belongs to the Lord Jesus Christ, he is the owner. Col 1:18 states, "*He is also head of the body, the church*; and He is the beginning, the firstborn from the dead, so that He himself will come to have first place in everything" (emphasis mine). The owner of an organization in our world outlines the function and structure of the organization. God the Son owns the church; therefore, the only logical conclusion is that the church is to function per his commands, not our thoughts. What do the commands of Christ (the New Testament) outline for us to do in order to worship him rightly as his gathered local people each Lord's Day? We have established that the Lord Jesus governs his church both local and universal. We know that the church is built through the Word of God (Rom 10:17: "So faith *comes* from hearing, and hearing by the word of Christ" [emphasis mine]) through his Word. We are commissioned as his people to make disciples and teach them to "observe" all his commands. Therefore, it is clear that the Word of God's explicit statements concerning corporate worship as a local church and the examples seen in Scripture are to drive what a local church does each Lord's Day as they gather together. The following is a list from Scripture concerning the local church and her formation. It will serve as the evidence for the verdict concerning how a local church is operated.

A Local Church's Membership Includes Baptized Born Again Believers

Acts 2:41

So then, those who had received his word were baptized; and that day there were added about three thousand souls. They were continually devoting themselves to the apostles' teaching and to fellowship, to the breaking of bread and to prayer.[28]

Eph 2:4–5

But God, being rich in mercy, because of His great love with which He loved us, even when we were dead in our transgressions, made us alive together with Christ (by grace you have been saved), . . .[29]

---

28. Emphasis mine.
29. Emphasis mine.

Gather on the Lord's Day (Sunday, the first day of the week, which was the day the Lord Jesus rose from the dead)

ACTS 20:7

On the first day of the week, when we were gathered together to break bread, Paul *began* talking to them, intending to leave the next day, and *he prolonged his message until midnight.*[30]

REV 1:10

I was in the Spirit on the Lord's day, and I heard behind me a loud voice like *the sound* of a trumpet, . . .[31]

HEB 10:24–25

. . . and let us consider how to stimulate one another to love and good deeds, *not forsaking our own assembling together*, as is the habit of some, but encouraging *one another*; and all the more as you see the day drawing near.[32]

Practice Loving Church Discipline (Removal from Membership of Local Church)

MATT 18:15–20

If your brother sins, go and show him his fault in private; if he listens to you, you have won your brother. But if he does not listen to you, take one or two more with you,

---

30. Emphases mine.
31. Emphases mine.
32. Emphases mine.

so that by the mouth of two or three witnesses every fact may be confirmed. *If he refuses to listen to them, tell it to the church; and if he refuses to listen even to the church, let him be to you as a Gentile and a tax collector.* Truly I say to you, whatever you bind on earth shall have been bound in heaven; and whatever you loose on earth shall have been loosed in heaven.

Again I say to you, that if two of you agree on earth about anything that they may ask, it shall be done for them by My Father who is in heaven. For where two or three have gathered together in My name, I am there in their midst."[33]

1 Cor 5:4–5

In the name of our Lord Jesus, *when you are assembled,* and I with you in spirit, with the power of our Lord Jesus, I have *decided to deliver such a one to Satan* for the destruction of his flesh, *so that his spirit may be saved in the day of the Lord Jesus.*[34]

Reading the Word and Preaching the Word

1 Tim 4:13

Until I come, *give attention to the public reading of Scripture, to exhortation and teaching.*[35]

---

33. Emphasis mine.
34. Emphasis mine.
35. Emphasis mine.

True Worship

2 Tim 3:16–4:2

All Scripture is inspired by God and profitable for teaching, for reproof, for correction, for training in righteousness; so that the man of God may be adequate, equipped for every good work.

I solemnly charge you *in the presence of God and of Christ Jesus, who is to judge the living and the dead, and by His appearing and His kingdom:* preach the word; *be ready in season* and *out of season; reprove, rebuke, exhort, with great patience and instruction.*[36]

Sing the Word Congregationally

Eph 5:19

. . . speaking to one another in psalms and hymns and spiritual songs, singing and making melody with your heart to the Lord . . .[37]

Col 3:16

Let the word of Christ richly dwell within you, with all wisdom teaching and *admonishing one another with psalms and hymns and spiritual songs, singing with thankfulness in your hearts to God.*[38]

---

36. Emphases mine.
37. Emphasis mine.
38. Emphasis mine.

Pray per the Word (Prayers of Praise/Adoration, Confession with Assurance, and Thanksgiving)

1 Tim 2:1–2

First of all, then, *I urge that entreaties and prayers, petitions and thanksgivings, be made on behalf of all men,* for kings and all who are in authority, so that we may lead a tranquil and quiet life in all godliness and dignity.[39]

Eph 1:3

Blessed be the God and Father of our Lord Jesus Christ, who has blessed us with every spiritual blessing in the heavenly *places* in Christ, . . .[40]

1 John 1:9

If we confess our sins, He is faithful and righteous to forgive us our sins and to cleanse us from all unrighteousness.[41]

Col 3:17

Whatever you do in word or deed, *do* all in the name of the Lord Jesus, *giving thanks through Him to God the Father.*[42]

---

39. Emphasis mine.
40. Emphases mine.
41. Emphasis mine.
42. Emphases mine.

True Worship

Collect Tithes and Offerings to Support of the Work of the Word

1 Cor 16:1-4

Now concerning the collection for the saints, as I directed the churches of Galatia, so do you also. *On the first day of every week each one of you is to put aside and save*, as he may prosper, so that no collections be made when I come. When I arrive, whomever you may approve, I will send them with letters to carry your gift to Jerusalem; and if it is fitting for me to go also, they will go with me.[43]

1 Cor 9:13-14

I am not speaking these things according to human judgment, am I? Or does not the Law also say these things? For it is written in the Law of Moses, "You shall not muzzle the ox while he is threshing." God is not concerned about oxen, is He? Or is He speaking altogether for our sake? Yes, for our sake it was written, because the plowman ought to plow in hope, and the thresher to thresh in hope of sharing the crops. If we sowed spiritual things in you, is it too much if we reap material things from you? If others share the right over you, do we not more? Nevertheless, we did not use this right, but we endure all things so that we will cause no hindrance to the gospel of Christ. Do you not know that those who perform sacred services eat the food of the temple, and those who attend regularly to the altar have their share from the altar? *So also the Lord directed those who proclaim the gospel to get their living from the gospel.*[44]

---

43. Emphases mine.
44. Emphasis mine.

True Worship of God in Spirit and Truth

Baptism and Lord's Supper per the Word

Matt 28:19-20

Go therefore and make disciples of all the nations, *baptizing them in the name of the Father and the Son and the Holy Spirit,* teaching them to observe all that I commanded you; and lo, I am with you always, even to the end of the age.[45]

1 Cor 11:23-26

For I received from the Lord that which I also delivered to you, that the Lord Jesus in the night in which He was betrayed took bread; and when He had given thanks, He broke it and said, "This is My body, which is for you; do this in remembrance of Me." In the same way *He took* the cup also after supper, saying, *"This cup is the new covenant in My blood; do this, as often as you drink it, in remembrance of Me."* For as often as you eat this bread and drink the cup, you proclaim the Lord's death until He comes.[46]

A Plurality of Qualified Elders to Oversee the Local Church

Acts 14:23

When they had appointed elders for them in every church, having prayed with fasting, they commended them to the Lord in whom they had believed.[47]

---

45. Emphasis mine.
46. Emphases mine.
47. Emphasis mine.

True Worship

Titus 1:5

> For this reason I left you in Crete, that you would set in order what remains and *appoint elders in every city as I directed you.*[48]

1 Tim 3:1-6

> It is a trustworthy statement: if any man aspires to the office of overseer, it is a fine work he desires *to do. An overseer, then, must be above reproach, the husband of one wife, temperate, prudent, respectable, hospitable, able to teach, not addicted to wine or pugnacious, but gentle, peaceable, free from the love of money. He must be one who manages his own household well, keeping his children under control with all dignity (but if a man does not know how to manage his own household, how will he take care of the church of God?),* and not a new convert, so that he will not become conceited and fall into the condemnation incurred by the devil. And he must have a good reputation with those outside the church, so that he will not fall into reproach and the snare of the devil.[49]

The Verdict—What the True Worship of God in the Local Church Looks Like (It is a People and Service that is Regulative in Principle because it is Word-Centered in Nature)

The verdict is in. Many courtrooms have a moment of tense silence when that reality hits. The idea is this: the evidence has been presented and examined, and now comes the conclusion and summation of the matter at hand. The Scriptures have been put forth (the evidence). Now comes the conclusion (the verdict) concerning

---

48. Emphasis mine.
49. Emphasis mine.

how the local church is to operate and what it is to do in the Sunday Lord's Day service. (The reason it is the Lord's Day is it follows the example of the local church, such as in Acts 20:7 and Rev 1:10). Remember again for a moment what we have learned about what a local church is. The New Testament local church gathers together to worship the triune God as his redeemed around his Word. The local church service is not permitted to approach God our own way, doing our own thing. Rather, the church is primarily about ascribing to God glory per his instructions in his Word. From the outlined Scriptures we come to a clear picture of how a church is to operate per the regulative principle (the church only does what Scripture commands or shows). The conclusion is in. Here it is.

The local church is centered on the preached Word of God by qualified elders. The church is to be cared for by a plurality of qualified elders who know the Word and are able to rightly explain it. The local church gathers each Lord's Day to hear the Word preached book by book, verse by verse. The preaching pastor proclaims the meaning of the Scripture expositionally (the theme of the sermon is derived from the meaning of the text preached) and lovingly applies it to the local church gathered.

Congregationally, the local church sings rich, theologically accurate hymns and spiritual songs, as well as the Psalms. The singing portion of the service is not to be a concert with gifted people being admired for their performance ability on the stage. The singing portion of the Scripture is an "admonishing one another" type of setting where we as the congregation sing out the rich truths of Scripture in worship to the triune God we love, as well as for our mutual edification in the Lord Jesus. It is the entire congregational singing out the doctrines of the holy Scriptures.

The local church reads the Scriptures. We should read Scripture to open service and begin focusing our mind on and seeing our affections stirred for the sovereign God who saves sinners. We read Scriptures during the service highlighting the various truths about God and our need for the gospel of grace. We focus on God's attributes and the doctrines of the faith from the Scripture we read through the service.

True Worship

The local church prays corporately. The local body engages in prayers of praise, confession, thanksgiving, intercession, supplication, etc. We lift up other churches and our civic leaders. We pray for unreached people groups and needs. The idea is that our Scripture readings as well as prayers should be so potent and at times a tad lengthy that nominal Christians are driven out of the fellowship or towards true fellowship with the Lord Jesus. We close with scriptural benedictions that highlight the attributes of God, the gospel, and God's covenantal love for his people.

The local church partakes of the Lord's Supper as local church members in good standing. The local church observes the ordinance of baptism for born again Christians entering into the membership of the local church.

Local churches practice regenerate (born again) membership whereby the elders review candidates for membership to ensure they have the fruit of salvation from the root of knowing/professing the gospel and present such people to the congregation to affirm in an assembled meeting (normally a business meeting).

The local church practices loving church discipline, of which the final step is the removal of a person's membership as well as their access to the Lord's Supper table, all for the protection of the church and the good of the offender (baptism being the front door of membership and the Lord's Supper guarding the back door).

The local church is to take up an offering to support the work of the ministry of the Word, the needs of the church, as well as the Great Commission.

As we do these things, we encounter the glory of God, and are increasingly conformed into the image of God, and ascribe to God rightly praise due to his name. In essence the local church is to be the place where the doctrine of the sufficiency of Scripture is seen in everything read, said, prayed, preached, and practiced. We worship God in spirit as his Holy-Spirit-indwelled and redeemed people per his Word. Remember in his Word alone we see the triune God revealed to us in his attributes. A service regulated by the Word of God should move God's genuine sheep to awe and wonder at the glory of God and the weight of his majesty as they encounter him each Lord's Day. This is the type of corporate setting that truly worships God in spirit and truth. A Word-based local church is a Spirit-led, truth-loving church that worships God rightly. *See appendix 1 for three examples of regulative church services from Christ Church Radford, Capitol Hill Baptist Church, and First Baptist Church Puxico.*

Worship in Spirit and Truth

Jesus told the Samaritan women that the Father is calling forth a people who will worship him in spirit and truth. Individually as Christians and corporately as local churches, this means we are Holy-Spirit-indwelled people who by God's grace are governed in all we do according to the truth of God's Word. We are people who come to the Father through Jesus alone. We are people who worship God per his Word alone. We are people who not only proclaim the Reformation battle call of "*sola scriptura*"; we live it out. For in the Scriptures alone we find the God of glory who alone satisfies his people to the eternal utmost, and he is worthy of true worship.

Discussion Questions

1. What does it mean to worship God in spirit and truth?
2. What does it mean personally as a Christian to worship God in spirit and truth?
3. What does it mean corporately as a local church to worship God in spirit and truth?

Appendix 1: Service Orders of Regulative Worship Churches

Example 1: Christ Church at Radford, VA Service Order[1]

Call to Order
Scripture Reading. Prayer Talk.
Song
Corporate Prayer Meeting (45 minutes)
Closing Prayer/Break
Call to Worship (Portion of Scripture Read)
Song (Corporate Singing)
Pastoral Prayer
Scripture Reading (in context)
Song
Preaching
Benediction
Fellowship Meal

---

1. Used with the permission of the pastors of the church.

APPENDIX 1

Example 2: Capitol Hill Baptist Church, Washington, DC Service Order[2]

Order of Service, February 2, 2020
"We gather this morning to praise our sovereign God."
Welcome
Scriptural Call to Worship Ps 149
The Lord's Prayer
Hymn "Christ, the Sure and Steady Anchor"
Hymn "Come, Ye Sinners (I Will Arise)"
Hymn "All Glory Be to Christ"
Prayer of Praise
Antiphonal Scripture Reading 1 Tim 2:1–8
Prayer of Confession and Scriptural Assurance of Pardon
    Eph 2:8
Children in kindergarten through third grade participating in Praise Factory should exit during this hymn:
Hymn "Ah, Holy Jesus, How Hast Thou Offended"
Pastoral Prayer of Petition
Hymn "My Worth Is Not in What I Own"
Prayer of Thanks
Offertory
Message

> Ezra 6
> The Nation Refounded
> Worship Renewed

Hymn "Afflicted Saint, to Christ Draw Near"
Silence for Reflection and Preparation: After the benediction, we will spend the next few moments silently reflecting on our time together this morning. When the piano resumes to mark the conclusion of the service, we invite all to stay around for conversation; refreshments are provided throughout the building.

---

2. Used with the permission of the pastors of the church.

APPENDIX 1

Example 3: First Baptist Puxico Service Order[3]

Welcome
"We're glad you decided to worship with us this morning as we celebrate the coming of our Savior. If you are a guest, please fill out the welcome tab attached and place it in the offering plate or in the basket on the Welcome Center."
Call to Worship—Ps 95
Opening Prayer—Prayer of Confession and Assurance of Forgiveness
Congregational Singing
      "Crown Him with Many Crowns"
      "O Mighty Cross"
      "Christ is All"
Congregational Giving
Preaching God's Word
      1 Cor 10–11:1
Song of Response
"I Will Wait for You (Ps 130)"
Benediction—Eph 3:20–21
Closing Prayer—Prayer of Thanksgiving

---

3. Used with the permission of the pastors of the church.

Appendix 2:
Recommended Resources for Further Study

Below is a short list of books that further evaluate this topic of biblical worship.

Daily Worship of God

Piper, John. *Desiring God: Meditations of a Christian Hedonist*. Rev. ed. Colorado Springs: Multnomah, 2011.

Piper, John. *Pleasures of God: Meditations on God's Delight in Being God*. 2nd ed. Colorado Springs: Multnomah, 2000.

Corporate Worship of God

Dever, Mark. *Nine Marks of Healthy Church*. 3rd ed. Wheaton, IL: Crossway, 2013.

Dever, Mark, and Paul Alexander. *The Deliberate Church: Building Your Ministry on the Gospel*. Wheaton, IL: Crossway, 2005.

Kauflin, Bob. *Worship Matters: Leading Others to Encounter the Greatness of God*. Wheaton, IL: Crossway, 2008.

Other Related Resources

Sproul, Robert C. *The Holiness of God*. Rev. ed. Carol Stream, IL: Tyndale, 2000.

Washer, Paul David. *Ten Indictments Against the Modern Church*. Grand Rapids: Reformation Heritage, 2018.

Appendix 2

Grudem, Wayne. *Christian Beliefs: Twenty Basics Every Christian Should Know.* Edited by Elliot Grudem. Grand Rapids: Zondervan, 2005.

Calvin, John. *The Institutes of the Christian Religion.* Edited by Robert White. Edinburgh: Banner of Truth, 2014.

Baxter, Richard. *Gildas Salvianus: The Reformed Pastor.* Edited by John T. Wilkinson. Eugene, OR: Wipf & Stock, 2018.

Bibliography

Barker, Kenneth L., and John R. Kohlenberger III. *The Expositor's Bible Commentary: Abridged Edition*. Vol. 2, *New Testament*. Grand Rapids: Zondervan, 1994.

Manser, Martin H. et al. *Zondervan Dictionary of Bible Themes: An Accessible and Comprehensive Tool for Topical Studies*. Grand Rapids: Zondervan, 1999.

"Mega Churches Offer Prayer, Play, and Shopping." *ABC News*, January 6, 2006. https://abcnews.go.com/GMA/Business/story?id=617341&page=1.

Swanson, James A. *A Dictionary of Biblical Languages with Semantic Domains: Hebrew (OT)*. Bellingham, WA: Faithlife, 2001. Logos Software.

Walvoord, John F., and Roy B. Zuck, eds. *The Bible Knowledge Commentary: New Testament*. Bible Knowledge Series, vol. 2. Wheaton: Victor, 1985.

www.ingramcontent.com/pod-product-compliance
Lightning Source LLC
Chambersburg PA
CBHW070325100426
42743CB00011B/2564